Dedication

Happiness is when what you think,
what you say, and what you do are in harmony.

Mahatma Gandhi

This book is dedicated to all those who, seeking inner peace, discover
it at last within them and to those who help us, by their own being
and art, to get there.

This is a work of fiction. The characters are figments of my
imagination. The recipes are real, though.

WR

Acknowledgements

My grateful thanks, as always, to all who have supported and helped me to put together this book. Especially, I want to thank the following:

John McMahon, for sharing stories and providing the spark that lit the idea

Robin Harnish, for creating the recipes and for all her dedication to the principles within this book

Debbie Elicksen, for ordering the words in such a way that they mean something, and for taking the burden of managing the book's production

Bobbie-Jo Bergner, for her wonderful energy in providing the design elements

My daughter Josie, for the poem she wrote over thirty years ago and that now appears as part of Jenny's story

For all of you, too many to name, who have been engaged with me in the journey to Emotional Fitness and inner peace over the past ten years in Calgary – and before that in England

To the amazing teachers, most long gone, who brought me to my own self-actualization and inner peace

And finally, as ever, to my wife Nicole Tremblay, whose support, challenge, and above all love, is the inspiration in my life

Recipes for Inner Peace

Warren Redman

Author of the Award-Winning

The 9 Steps to Emotional Fitness

With recipes by
Robin Harnish

Here are some
yummy recipes
for your tummy.
and some food
for your thought!
Hugs, JoAnn

Library and Archives Canada Cataloguing in Publication

Redman, Warren
Recipes for Inner Peace / Warren Redman; Editor, Debbie Elicksen.
ISBN 0-9699189-2-5
1. Self-actualization (Psychology). I. Elicksen, Debbie II. Title.

BF637.S4R436 2005 158.1 C2005-904960-X

Publisher
Merlin Star Press

Calgary, Alberta, Canada

www.RecipesforInnerPeace.com

Production: Debbie Elicksen
Cover & Internal Design: Bobbie-Jo Bergner, Mind's Design Studio
Front Cover Photo: Jeff Dykes, Flash World of Stock
Back/Side Cover Heart Photo: Ellen Isaacs, Flash World of Stock
Recipes: Robin Harnish

Printing
Houghton Boston
Saskatoon, SK, Canada

Recipes for Inner Peace – 2nd Edition
Printed and Bound in Canada
Copyright 2005

FOREWORD

I believe it was in the fall 2004, when I was having coffee with Warren Redman. His friends will picture the scene. Nursing a steaming cup of dark roast and nibbling on a muffin at The Joshua Tree café. Conversation flowing like Calgary's rain-swollen Bow River in flood. Challenge: how to get the word of Emotional Fitness out to more people, to make it a household word? And voila, why not write a cookbook?

Well as anyone who has waited for a good meal knows, anticipation and kitchen smells are at least half the fun. I have been re-reading his other books lately, before bedtime. Snacking on the little tidbits of the main course that cook allows me to steal. But then along came last night, when I received the manuscript for *Recipes for Inner Peace*. Suffice it to say, I couldn't put the mouse down. (I love computers). Guilty as charged of binge reading! I was taken on a brief and succulent voyage that explains the nine steps to Emotional Fitness and a number of delicious meals that have been concocted by chef Robin Harnish. Yes, this book will literally and physically feed your body and soul. That is the fun and privilege for those lucky enough to do coffee with Warren. Eating, drinking and moving through pain to pleasure, through doubt to certainty, through lassitude to energetic action: all things that a well nourished mind and body can achieve. I have had the main course, Personal Coaching with Warren that has opened up previously undreamed of vistas. Thank heavens I pulled my chair up to the table.

So, enjoy your feast. Eat and drink well, fill your body and soul courtesy this most delicious offering.

John McMahon

Calgary Alberta

Contents:

1. Introduction
Let's start with Desserts

*The greatest journey begins
with many setbacks.
They are the sparks that ignite
the fuel to carry you forward.*

This book has to begin with desserts. Most cookbooks don't start that way, especially those aimed at healthy eating. But this book is about healthy <u>being</u>, not just healthy living or healthy eating. First, just to get you into the mood and show you we mean business, write down desserts backwards (that is, from right to left). Go on (unless you haven't yet bought this book) write it now on this page.

_____

Do you feel like this sometimes? Do you prefer to have it the other way round? Are you one of those people who eat desserts when you're stressed? What fascinating arrangement of the lexicon decreed that the two words are an exact opposite?

. . . .

Jenny loved her desserts. She loved making them, and she loved eating them – the sweeter and stickier, the better. She couldn't get enough of them. She never missed having a dessert after her evening meal. Sometimes, she crept downstairs in the middle of the night and helped herself to leftover pie or chocolate cake. And it showed.

As much as she loved her desserts, Jenny hated her weight. Worse than that, she hated the guilt she felt as she bit into the last morsel. She hated how she felt standing alone in the dark and midnight silence of the kitchen as she opened the refrigerator door. The guilt came in the form of voices inside her head – voices of her family and friends scolding her for being fat. Strangely, she could not recall anyone actually saying that to her, but it sure felt like it.

One Thursday morning in November, Jenny broke down. Her boss called her into his office and barely started to speak, when an overwhelming sense of hopelessness came over her. Her boss blamed her for something she had or hadn't done. He obviously thought she was useless. Her parents were disappointed in her inability to make something of her life. She never managed to develop a lasting relationship with any man who offered her genuine love. Even her friends saw her as a loser. Suddenly, Jenny realized her desserts were just a substitute for what she really wanted in her life but thought she could never have. She felt ashamed and desperately unhappy. In front of her boss, who still appeared to be talking without her hearing a word, she sobbed like a small child whose world had just come to an end because her favorite toy was lost.

Jenny's boss didn't know what to do at first. He handed her a box of tissues and told her everything was going to be all right. He asked if she would like to take a couple of days off and suggested she might like to talk to someone. Through her sniffles, Jenny asked what he meant.

"I mean it seems you could do with a little break and someone who could help you to sort out whatever seems to be troubling you," said her boss. "I think I know just the person. He's about to come and see me in the next couple of minutes. He's my personal coach. I'd like to introduce you to him." Jenny's boss leant forward and lowered his voice, although nobody could possibly have heard them talking, since the office door was closed. "I tell you what," he said, "As a way to show I really want to support you Jenny, I'll pay for a couple of sessions, just so you can see how helpful it can be to talk to someone like Nicolas."

The following Monday morning, Jenny found herself talking with Nicolas as she had talked with nobody else before. He described himself as an Emotional Fitness coach. He seemed to do very little except listen to her. But he listened in a way she had never experienced. She heard herself in a new way. She began to hear her own voice, not the voices of others. She began to understand what she was doing because she had not believed in herself. Nicolas told her nothing, gave her no advice, offered no criticism. And yet, Jenny saw that she had it all backwards. She was stressed and responded with desserts.

For the first time in many years, Jenny felt hope. She understood her addiction was a response to her feelings of inadequacy. Now she knew she could change those feelings once she really learned to listen to herself.

At the end of her first session with Nicolas, she made two commitments. The first was to continue to see him every week, whether her boss paid for it or not. The second was that she wouldn't deprive herself of her desserts, but she'd make something healthier and less fattening.

. . . .

The man sat on a window-stool in the small dessert and coffee bar that was one of his favorite Calgary haunts, toying with a strawberry cheesecake and sipping at a large caffeine-loaded black coffee. Today was his thirty-fifth birthday, and this was his birthday party.

He gazed out through the window at the people passing by in the darkness, their quick strides taking them away from their work in the cold November air to some warm and inviting place.

Serge dipped his fork into the cheesecake, pulled a morsel towards his mouth, and made a sudden decision. Next year, he would not do this – not alone anyway. This was as good a time as any to review where he was, what he was doing, and what he wanted to do with the rest of his life. The only thing he knew for sure was that being alone didn't feel too wonderful any more.

Staring into the deep darkness of his coffee, Serge saw an eye peering back at him, inviting him, or so it seemed, to take a look at himself. He reflected on his life. It wasn't so bad. He had a good career, and the corporation rewarded him well for his work. Engineering had always fascinated him. He knew his skills were in high demand. The people at work were friendly, although most of them were married and busy with their young families. He got on well with his boss and enjoyed the challenges of the different projects that were entrusted to him. If he had his way, Serge would like to get his teeth into one of the longer-term programs, but those usually went to the more senior people. He supposed he'd have to wait, unless he moved to another company, which he didn't want to do. Yes, work was pretty good.

He missed his family and friends from home. Home was back east in Toronto. He especially missed his sister and her kids. They had a great relationship, but in the three years since he was in Calgary, he had seen them maybe four times. Without a steady relationship, he felt lonely. He'd had a few girlfriends, but nobody he could call special or who seemed attracted enough to him to want to go out for more than a couple of dates. After Sylvie refused to move west with him, he realized she wasn't the right one for him anyway. He was almost relieved she'd decided to stay in Toronto.

So now what? Serge finished his coffee and picked at the last of the crumbs left on his plate. Is this what life had to offer him, a few crumbs? No, it wasn't good enough. Something would change. If he only knew how to change it.

The stress-free dessert
Blueberry Crumble

It is the first of August in Nova Scotia: blueberry season! Plump high bush berries are used for this delicious dessert. This recipe has been redesigned to promote a low fat, refined sugar-free dish. As Jenny is changing her lifestyle, it is important that we all look at what we are eating. Changing recipes to suit our personal needs can be an activity that has its rewards.   RH

Recipe designed for 4-6 servings

Base:
5 cups blueberries
2 tb. honey
1 cinnamon stick
1 tb. fresh ginger, grated
1 lemon, juice
2 tb. apple juice or water

Topping:
1 cup flour
2 cups rolled quick oats
½ tsp baking powder
Pinch sea salt
½ cup almonds, finely chopped
½ cup sunflower oil (or other light oil)
½ cup maple syrup

Method:

1. In a medium sized saucepan, heat 3 cups blueberries, maple syrup, cinnamon, ginger, lemon, and water. Simmer on medium heat for 10 minutes.

2. Add remaining blueberries. Mix cornstarch with water and stir for about another minute. Remove from heat and pour into an ovenproof dish.

3. For the topping: mix flour, oats, baking powder, salt, and almonds in a bowl. Add oil and maple syrup and mix until combined. Gently place over blueberries.

4. Bake uncovered in preheated oven at 350⁰F for 25 minutes. The topping will sink a bit, as it is soaked up by the blueberries, but that is the best part! Eat warm with cold cream or vanilla ice cream.

2. Listen to yourself
Soul food

Know yourself first.
When you truly accept who you are,
you have taken your first step to
fulfillment.

"I wish I knew what makes me want to binge. I just hate myself for doing that."

Jenny sat in an easy chair facing Nicolas in his light and comfortable office. It was just after four in the afternoon of the second weekly session that Jenny had booked with her coach. On his suggestion, she agreed to ten such sessions. Last week, her first, Jenny left feeling lighter and clearer than she had felt for, probably, ever. It wasn't that she didn't have a thousand questions. She wondered why she hadn't sought this kind of help before. She wondered how Nicolas helped her without ever seeming to offer any advice or answers.

"Jenny," said Nicolas, his quiet baritone voice providing a sense of safety and comfort, "we can find out what makes you binge, as you put it. We can also change the feeling that you hate yourself. But what I would like to do at this point is to help you to listen to yourself properly. Is that something you'd like to do?"

Jenny leant forward. "I'd certainly like to learn to listen like you do," she answered, "but how do I listen to myself? It seems like such a mess inside my head. There are so many different voices in there telling me what to do. It drives me crazy."

Nicolas smiled. "That's exactly what we need to sort out. You can learn to distinguish between the voices that are not yours and the one that is truly, authentically you. That's the one to trust."

It seemed to Jenny as though a light had been switched on. It illuminated an image of her listening to voices that didn't belong to her. She pictured her parents, well-meaning and always wanting the best from her. They pushed her into doing things as a child that she never really wanted. Almost daily, she heard her father inside her head telling her to stand up for herself, her mother saying she should take better care of herself. At this very moment, she could hear her dad telling her that seeing a personal coach showed weakness and her mom worrying about her weight. They didn't say those things to her in reality. They didn't need to. Which was her true voice? What did she really think? Who was she?

She looked up at Nicolas. "Yes," she said. "I want to learn to listen to me, because what I really want is to have some inner peace."

"Then I'll introduce you to Listening Power," Nicolas continued. "It's the first and most important recipe in the nine that I'm going to show you over the next few weeks. If you learn just this, you will have the power to make life better than you ever imagined and to have that inner peace you seek. There are two things you need to understand, two things that get in the way of us listening fully. The first is us. By that, I mean we get in the way of being able to listen properly. The second thing is we don't know how because nobody ever showed us. I am going to show you. You must promise to practice it with others and with yourself."

"I promise," responded Jenny without hesitation. "I really promise."

"Then you have already mastered the first stage of listening," said Nicolas. "The first stage is what I call setting a contract. When you consciously say to yourself, or to someone else, that you will listen fully, you have come to an agreement that sets the scene for listening to take place."

"You mean it's as easy as that?"

"Well, it sounds easy, and it really is that simple. The sad thing is it hardly ever happens, except in settings like this. Normally, we don't listen to each other or to ourselves because we never get to the first stage of deciding that's what we'll do."

Jenny frowned. "So what do I do? I mean, how do I make a contract with myself?"

"I'll give you some idea, but you have to do what feels the best to you. Take some time during the day when you can have some private space. Make yourself comfortable and see that you're not interrupted or diverted by anything or anyone else. Decide how long you will spend concentrating on yourself – say twenty minutes or so. Simply say, out loud, that you are going to listen to yourself without any judgment. You will trust yourself to listen as best you can. Do you think you can do that?"

Jenny began to feel uncertain. "But what if I start getting negative thoughts? I'll just go round in circles and not be able to get out. I'll make it worse."

"You're jumping ahead, Jenny. Can you see what you've done? You have already decided it won't work before you start. You have set yourself up to fail before you have even made a contract with yourself."

Jenny squirmed uncomfortably in her chair. She had made a promise, and now she didn't feel like keeping it. She didn't want to do this. It sounded too difficult. She just wanted the pain to go away. She felt as though Nicolas would judge her, think she was stupid or weak if she backed down. She glanced at him. He waited calmly, his hands resting lightly on his knees. The silence hung heavily in the air. She noticed she had stopped breathing and inhaled deeply, letting the breath out slowly.

In that moment, she began to understand. She heard the messages inside her head, or somewhere, telling her what she should and shouldn't do. Suddenly, she saw that most of her behavior was an attempt to do what she thought other people expected. Then she became upset. To compensate, she indulged herself by eating unhealthily.

She looked directly at Nicolas. "Yes, I can do it," she replied slowly, as though to herself. "I realize I try to second guess what others are thinking. I sabotage myself by doing what I believe they want instead of what I want. Now I don't even know what I want. I was going to say to you, Nicolas, I would do what you ask because I thought you'd be annoyed with me if I didn't. You would think I was stupid, even though I didn't feel like doing it. Now I want to do it because I see how important it is. I think I'm listening to myself already."

Nicolas gave her a broad smile. "You certainly are. In fact, you are already moving to the second stage of Listening Power, which is to focus on what is important. Once you have made a contract with yourself, you need to discover what you want to select from all your thoughts and feelings. For example, you could focus on the first comment you made today, about wanting to understand your bingeing and how you hate it. Or you could decide to concentrate on the question about what you want."

"How do I find one thing out of all the jumble that goes on in my head?"

"I'm not saying it's easy. It needs lots of practice. What's important is to trust yourself to identify and focus on one of those things from the jumble. Everything is connected, of course, but when you concentrate on one thing at a time and go through the other stages I will tell you about, you will find that everything starts to get much clearer. You will become your own best Emotional Fitness coach."

Jenny was uncertain again. Could she do this herself? Then she realized she would not be doing it alone. She could learn to be her own coach if she had the support of Nicolas, who would teach her. An unfamiliar surge of warmth trickled through her. It dawned on her that it was a feeling of confidence. She had almost forgotten what it felt like.

"What do I do when I focus on something that I want to deal with?" she asked.

"The third stage in Listening Power is to understand what your thoughts and feelings mean." Nicolas leant back in his chair and closed his eyes.

Jenny waited, wondering if he'd gone to sleep. Maybe the session was over. She looked at her watch. Twenty minutes left. She relaxed. Something would happen. She was beginning to enjoy this.

Nicolas opened his eyes and continued speaking as though nothing had happened. "Remember, Jenny, to suspend any judgment about yourself or anyone else. Ask yourself questions. For example, if you are focusing on your eating, what do you feel when you eat unhealthily? Explore what inner voices you hear. Maybe you would ask yourself what you mean when you say you hate yourself. Avoid asking the question why. That seldom has a helpful answer and tends not to take you forward. You are doing the best you can to understand your own voice by asking questions. That helps you become clearer and make connections between the various thoughts you have. It's like one of those games where you connect the dots to reveal a picture."

Jenny recalled the children's books she used to own with the word and picture puzzles. She enjoyed those. She used to paint too. She suddenly longed to do something creative again. It had been years since she'd picked up a paintbrush. What did she do with her creativity?

"I think I have just connected a couple of dots," she told Nicolas. "I don't do anything for myself or anything I really enjoy. I used to love painting. I miss it, but I haven't thought about it for years. I let too much get in the way." She stopped abruptly, believing she had taken Nicolas away from his point. "I'm sorry. I don't know why that came up. It was your talk about the picture game, I guess."

"It's perfect Jenny," Nicolas replied. "You are making this work for you. You see how you can be your own best coach?"

He took a sip of the water that stood in a glass at his side. "Now Jenny, once you have connected the dots, or as many as you can, we come to the next stage in Listening Power. You have set your contract, you have focused on what is important for you, and you have done your best to understand the meaning of your thoughts and feelings. Now, you will pull it all together and describe the essence of what you have said. It's like making a summary of the main points, or if you prefer to stick to the painting analogy, like looking at the picture of what you have drawn now that the dots are connected."

"I get it." Jenny felt almost breathless now. "I remember always being so surprised as a kid when I connected the dots and suddenly at the end was the picture of a horse or something. So what do I do then?"

"Wow, you are moving fast. You've just arrived at the last stage of Listening Power."

Jenny looked bemused. "What do you mean?"

"I mean when you are satisfied with the picture you have drawn or the summary you have made, your final stage is to answer the question 'what do I do now?' In other words, you are moving to some kind of action. If you drew a picture of a real horse, you could decide to jump on it and ride off." Nicolas looked pleased at the quirkiness of this idea. "On the other hand," he quickly asserted, "you are more likley to have come to some other conclusion. In fact, Jenny, you may have decided on an action point while we have been talking about this. Any thoughts about that?"

It didn't take Jenny long to answer.

"I am sure about one thing. I want to paint. I realize I miss it. I miss a whole creative side of myself. Is that what you mean?"

"That's a wonderful start, Jenny. Even without going through the process out loud, you have discovered an important part of yourself that has been hiding. Will you bring something in to show me next week?"

Once more, she felt a sense of doubt. Next week? Would she be able to do something by then? He was pushing her. She knew she was resisting because she was uncertain whether she could paint anything worthy of showing him. Time was up now. She didn't want it to end with her feeling like this. Why did he have to make it so difficult for her? Jenny stooped to pick up her purse. As she did, a surge of energy ran through her. She sat back in her chair. "Yes, I'll paint something and bring it."

While standing, Nicolas picked up a sheet of paper from the small table beside him and handed it to Jenny. "This is for you – a reminder of the five stages of Listening Power. See how you get on practicing them during the week. I'm looking forward to hearing how you did and to seeing your painting. I want you to know that whatever you paint will be perfect. The important thing will be that you bring out that part of you that has been missing for so long."

As Jenny walked away from his office, she noticed again her step seemed lighter, her head clearer, and her shoulders straighter.

. . . .

The atmosphere in the bar was noisy, brash, and crowded. Serge could hardly hear himself think, let alone hear the conversation around the table. He let the noise wash over him and allowed his eyes to take in the group.

Nine of them sat squashed at a table meant for eight. He felt like the odd man out, the ninth one. These were, he supposed, his friends. Three of them were from work, three were regulars at the bar who had joined them, and two were visitors from Montreal, who were the reason for this night out – although Serge hadn't figured out why or who they were attached to. He was squeezed between Grant, who worked in the cubicle that sufficed for an office next to his, and Ellie, a young woman – a regular patron – who often took time to talk with Serge.

The only way to have a conversation was to speak almost directly into the person's ear. He and Ellie engaged in a bizarre head dance.

"I've never seen you with a girl," bellowed Ellie. "Don't you have a regular date?"

"No," roared Serge. "Do you?"

"Not since my boyfriend, or ex-boyfriend, decided to take off for Vancouver and not come back," she shouted back.

Serge knew what his next move was supposed to be. Maybe it was as easy as this. Just sit in a bar until some girl made it plain that all you had to do was ask her out. He leant toward her, pointing his mouth at her waiting ear. "I hope it works out for you," he called. "You'll have to excuse me. I have to go now."

The fresh, sharp air hit him as he emerged from the bar. Serge knew better than to drive home. He hailed a cab. He was more alone than ever. He didn't want to go out with just any woman, not even one as attractive as Ellie. The unsettling thing was, as he engaged in the verbal fencing match with her, the image of another woman came into his mind. They went out on a date some time back. While it hadn't gone well, there was something about her he really liked.

He'd look up her number when he got home. He'd invite her to a nice quiet restaurant. He was glad he decided to listen to himself for a change, rather than going along for the ride with everyone else. It wasn't too late to call Jenny this evening.

Recipe for Listening Power

1. Set a contract where you will listen to yourself.

2. Focus on what's important right now.

3. Ask yourself what you mean. Connect the dots.

4. Summarize the essence of your meanings.
    Look at the overall picture.

5. What do you do with this? Decide upon your best action.

Food for the soul

Fresh Halibut with Kale and Ginger Baked in Parchment with Organic Brown Rice

When I think of nourishing my soul, the very first food that comes to mind is organic short grain brown rice! Mmm! Nothing feels nicer and more comforting! Veggies and fish work well together with this dish. I always feel so good after eating this meal. Kind of like Jenny when she left Nicolas' office after learning about Listening Power. Lighter, clearer, and happier. Enjoy!   RH

Recipe designed for 4-5 servings.

½ cup carrot, sliced thin into ½ moons
¼ cup celery, sliced on the bias thin
¼ cup red onion, sliced into thin slices
1 tsp. fresh thyme, minced or ½ tsp. dried
2 tb. ginger, grated
2 tb. lemon juice
3 tb. olive oil
1 tsp. sea salt
½ tsp. ground pepper
1 small bunch kale, stem and ribs removed, thinly sliced
4 6-oz. portions halibut or other white fish
¼ cup vegetable or chicken stock
¼ cup white wine
2 cups organic short grain brown rice
4 cups filtered water

Method:

1. Preheat oven to 400ºF. Cut 4 pieces of parchment paper to measure 14 x 16.

2. Stir together carrots, celery, red onion, thyme, ginger, lemon juice, oil, salt, pepper, and kale in a large bowl.

3. Season halibut with salt and pepper.

Continue...

4. Bring 4 cups of water to boil, add rinsed rice and reduce heat. Cover and cook 35-40 minutes.

5. Lay parchment rectangles on work surface. Place one halibut fillet on each parchment, divide kale equally, and place on top of halibut.

6. Working with one at a time, gather paper around filling to form a bundle; loosely tie with kitchen twine leaving a small opening.

7. Stir stock and white wine together and add about 2-3 tb. to each parcel. Tie twine in a bow to tightly seal.

8. Transfer bundles to a rimmed baking sheet. Bake 15-20 minutes. Transfer packets to plate or bowl and serve with brown rice.

3. Understanding others
Dinner for two

Attend fully to your friend's story and your enemy's alike. When you listen without getting in the way, you give and receive the greatest gift of love, where Mars and Venus finally meet.

The raw chill of the early December air seeped through Jenny's open coat as she stepped onto the sidewalk. She wrapped the material around her, tied the belt, and shivered slightly. Her third coaching session completed, she hurried to her car, anticipating the evening ahead of her with a mixture of pleasure and anxiety.

What good timing. This was the evening she had invited Serge to have dinner at her home. It was the first time in months she dared to do such a thing. Today's talk with Nicolas was great preparation. She had known Serge for nearly two years, but they usually saw each other in the company of others. Once, about six months ago, they went on a date together: a meal at a noisy restaurant bar, followed by a movie, and then a quiet drink in the lounge of a hotel. The evening finally ended with some awkward kissing before she fumbled her way out of his car and into her house.

She still felt embarrassed, but she liked Serge. She was glad he'd approached her again for a date to a quieter restaurant. She was even more pleased, if a little shocked, at her suggestion that instead she make dinner for him.

Jenny was proud of her cooking abilities, and was determined to cook and eat more healthily. Cooking for Serge would challenge her to be especially observant and creative about making a meal that was healthy and satisfying – maybe even enticing.

What she was less certain about was how to create a pleasing conversation with Serge. She found him passive. She herself was naturally withdrawn in the company of a man and compensated by talking what she felt was nonsense much of the time. How was she ever going to have a real relationship if she couldn't have a satisfying conversation?

These were the thoughts and questions she had put to Nicolas. He made it sound so easy.

"All you have to do," he said, "is to apply your Listening Power recipe to someone else."

Jenny looked back on their discussion as she drove the familiar route to her home. In a way, it was easy, and as Nicolas had pointed out, it was also hard because it seemed so unfamiliar. "It just takes lots of practice. Tonight is a wonderful time to start," he told her.

She went over the recipe. First, set up a contract. She laughed out loud in the safety and comfort of her vehicle as she pictured herself asking Serge to sign a legal document agreeing to how the evening would go. "Now sign here and here," she'd say, "and we can get on with dinner." Still smiling, she understood what Nicolas was getting at. This felt exciting and challenging. It meant having a healthy, adult interaction based on mutual respect and understanding.

The 'contract' was nothing less and nothing more than agreeing with Serge what they would both like from their time with each other, as openly and honestly as they could. If that scared Serge off, she would know he was not the kind of man she wanted to share time with. It didn't have to be difficult. She would start off, as she had rehearsed with Nicolas. She'd talk about some of the things she enjoyed in life while he listened to her. She would listen to him while he talked about anything important to him. She wouldn't interrupt him, although she might want to ask him more. She'd welcome him asking her questions about her own interests. She'd tell him she was trying to practice better communication and interaction and would like it if he felt able to take part with her. Jenny felt a flush of embarrassment. Could she really do this? What if Serge looked at her as though she were crazy and walked out? Was she crazy even to think about it? She recalled her previous attempts at relationships. She'd be crazy not to try it.

That was the first part of the recipe for creating a great relationship. If it got beyond that, what was next? Jenny had jotted down some notes, but she didn't need them now. She certainly didn't want to rummage in her briefcase while she was driving. She knew from her practice at listening to herself, the next stage was simply following on from the contract. She would invite Serge to talk about something that was important to him, something he felt comfortable sharing with her. If he wanted to talk about hockey, that would be okay. If he wanted to talk about his mother, fine. If he wanted to talk about his work, his hobby, his love of art, movies, and animals, or his dislike of children, cyclists, and crowds, she would hold back her own views and prejudices and simply hear him out. She'd get herself out of the way as much as she could. After all, if there was going to be any kind of a relationship between them, she wanted to know what was important to him. She wanted him to know about her. The contract would ensure they each had an equal share of the time.

Jenny suddenly wondered if this was going to be too serious to be fun. She didn't want to turn this into a joint therapy session or a debating society for two. It was a date. She'd mentioned this to Nicolas, who looked at her with his slightly quizzical expression and asked her why talking truthfully about things that interested them couldn't be fun. "It just seems a bit heavy," she responded. "I suppose if it's real, it will be okay. Come to think of it, when it's not real and when someone hogs the discussion, that's heavy. I want to run away. It's worth a go. All that can go wrong is I eat alone again."

Jenny turned the car onto her road and maneuvered it into her driveway. She turned off the motor and listened to the tick, tick, ticking of the engine as it cooled down quickly in the cold December air. The third stage in her recipe was simple or at least sounded simple. When Serge spoke, she would make sure she understood him. Without interrupting, she would ask a question if she was unclear. She might ask him to explain something a little more. She would make sure Serge knew she was focusing on him and what he was saying, and that she understood what he meant. She'd do her best to connect some of the things he said, so he really knew she was interested and wanted to get it – whatever it was.

A frown furrowed Jenny's brow. There were two more parts of this recipe. What were they? She began to reach for her briefcase, stopped, and sat back. "First I do this contract thing," she muttered under her breath. "Then invite him to talk about something that's important to him. Then show that I really want to understand. Oh, of course. Then I'll just tell Serge what I understood. What did Nicolas say? He talked about giving a gift. I'll give Serge the gift of knowing I understood him. Give him the picture of what I got. The last thing for the recipe mix was to ask him if there was anything he wanted to do that would take him forward, like something he'd want to change or do differently."

Jenny noticed her breath had steamed up the windshield. She gathered her things and flipped open the door. She was ready to cook dinner. She had the recipe for a successful date with Serge.

. . . .

"Hi Laurette. It's me, Serge."

His sister squealed into the phone. She never could hide her emotions, and he never wanted her to.

"Hi little brother, wonderful to hear your voice." She always called him little brother. His twin sister was nearly an hour older. Their characters were about as different as anyone could imagine. Laurette never seemed to spend time thinking about what had or hadn't happened; she just wanted to press ahead with life, take each moment as it came, and have fun with it. When they were young, she'd be the first one out in the snow to jump on the sled, while he made sure he wasn't going to get cold or get snow inside his boots. If it rained, she wanted to splash in the puddles; he skirted around them. When the sun came out, she'd want to play ball in the backyard; he would complain about having too much homework. On the other hand, Serge would listen to Laurette when she spilled her heart out to him about her various romantic encounters. On the rare occasion when he wanted to tell her about his girlfriend problems, she'd usually tell him not to be silly and ask another girl out. Serge loved his sister.

He realized he wanted to be a lot more like her, even though she exasperated him sometimes.

"Sis, I want to tell you about this evening I spent with a new lady I'm attracted to. I just want you to listen to me – not to give me any advice. Is that a deal?"

"Sure. As though I'd give you advice. Tell me about her. What's her name? How serious is this? It's about time you…oops! There I go. Shoot."

Serge felt the tension ease as his sister seemed to accept his request. He told Laurette about his dissatisfaction with his social life, how he'd called Jenny, and how the evening was so different. "She really wanted to know about me. I talked to her about things I never even knew I thought. I think she knows more about me than – well, even you. And then, the weird thing was, she asked me to listen to her the same way, and I did. We gave each other permission to say whatever we liked. It was really freeing. She seems so genuine and open. We were at her place. She made this great meal. I guess I'm feeling this is too good to be true,

Laurette. Can someone be such good company and a good cook without something being wrong? Am I missing something here?"

"Well, I don't know how to answer without giving advice. I think you better spend more time with her and find out. And Serge…"

"Yes?"

"Make sure you send her flowers. A girl like that has to be worth it – and deserves to know it."

Recipe for Understanding and Relationship-Building

1. Set up a contract that you will listen to each other. Make sure each person gets roughly the same time.

2. Focus on what's important right now for each person.

3. Ask the other person what s/he means. Connect the dots.

4. Summarize the essence of what you have understood. Look at the overall picture. Give the speaker the gift of showing you have listened and understood without making judgments.

5. Ask what the person wants to do with this. Help him or her to decide upon the best action.

The perfect dinner for two

When preparing this dinner, you may want to start the planning and preparation up to a week in advance. This ensures a relaxing evening for both you and your company.   RH

Cream of Carrot Soup

Carrots are listed as one of the first food that babies enjoy. Many parents give their very young children these healthy, vitamin-rich root vegetables. Cook the carrots well, on low heat, for up to an hour. Don't worry about loss of nutrients. They will all be in the broth. Puree well, and if trying to impress, strain through a mesh strainer before adding cream. This soup can be prepared a day in advance. Add cream when reheating.

This meal has been designed for 2-3 servings.

1 tb. butter
3 carrots, peeled and sliced
2 cloves garlic, crushed
1 small onion, diced
1-inch piece ginger, grated

½ tsp. ground cumin
½ tsp. cardamom, ground
Pinch nutmeg
3 cups vegetable stock
½ cup whipping cream

Method:

1.   In a medium saucepan, melt butter, add carrots, garlic, onion, and ginger, sweat for 5 minutes.

2.   Add spices and stir until fragrant.

3.   Add the vegetable stock and bring to a boil. Lower heat and simmer for 15 minutes, carrots should be soft.

4.   Puree soup until smooth, strain if desired.

5.   Keep warm until serving, whisk in cream and heat gently 1-2 minutes, serve.

Butter Leaf Salad with Avocado and Lime Yogurt Dressing

This light and refreshing salad can be prepared up to one hour before serving.

6 leaves butter leaf lettuce
½ avocado
1 mandarin orange, peeled and segmented
¼ cup pistachios, roasted 350°F for 8 minutes
½ cup plain yogurt
1 tsp. honey
1 tsp. limejuice
½ tsp. salt
½ tsp. white pepper
½ tsp. poppy seeds

Method:

1. Place butter leaf on a salad plate in an attractive pattern.

2. Cut avocado into 6 slices, removing skin. Place on plate.

3. Place half of the orange sliced on each plate in an attractive design.

4. Sprinkle pistachios around the plates.

5. Whisk yogurt, honey, limejuice, salt, pepper, and poppy seeds together in a small bowl.

6. Drizzle yogurt dressing over each salad and enjoy.

Seared Orange and Bourbon Salmon with Herbed Quinoa and Asparagus

'Searing' this salmon requires that you heat your pan up quite hot. Remove the salmon fillet from the marinade and pat dry with paper towel. Add about 1 tb. of oil to the pan and watch. It should heat up very quickly. Place your fillet belly side up. Do not move it for at least a good 5 minutes. When you turn your fillet over the top should have a lovely crust on it. This is the scrumptious part!   *RH*

¼ cup bourbon
2 tb. frozen orange juice concentrate
¼ cup tamari
¼ cup brown sugar
¼ cup chopped green onions
2 tb. fresh lemon juice
2 garlic cloves, minced
2 8-oz. salmon fillets

Method:

1.   Combine the first 7 ingredients in a large zip-lock bag and add salmon. Seal and marinate in refrigerator for 1-½ hours, turning the bag occasionally.

2.   Remove salmon from bag, discarding marinade. Heat saute pan on medium high heat add 1 tb. oil. Add fillets right away, belly side down. Sear the fish for 5-7 minutes without turning. Fish should get a bit of a crust from the natural caramelizing.

Herbed Quinoa

1½ cups quinoa, rinsed well
3 cups water or vegetable stock
½ tsp. salt
1 tsp. butter
2 tb. fresh chopped herbs (parsley, dill, basil, chives etc.)

Method:

1.   Bring water or stock to a rapid boil in medium saucepan.

2.   Add quinoa, salt, and butter. Lower heat to a simmer, cover and cook for 20 minutes.

3.   Remove from heat and rest for 5 minutes.

4.   To serve, stir in fresh herbs and fluff with a fork.

Steamed Asparagus

6 pieces fresh asparagus spears, bottoms cut and the bottom half peeled with a peeler
½ cup boiling water
½ tsp. salt

Method:

1.   Prepare asparagus.

2.   Bring water to boil in a wide shallow pan with lid, add salt.

3.   Blanch (steam) for 3-4 minutes.

Persian Poached Pears

2 large Bosc pears
1 cup water
1 cup dry white wine
2 tb. sugar
2 tb. honey
4 dried apricots
2 (3 x ½-inch) lemon rind strips
1 tsp. vanilla extract
1 whole clove
3 vanilla wafers, crushed
3 tb. roasted chopped pistachios

Method:

1. Peel and core pears, leaving stems intact. Slice about ¼ inch from base or each pear so it will sit flat.

2. Combine water and next 7 ingredients (water through cloves) in a large saucepan; bring to a boil.

3. Add pears, cover, reduce heat, and simmer for 10 minutes or until tender. Remove the pears and apricots from cooking liquid using a slotted spoon. Chill the pears and apricots.

4. Bring the liquid to a boil and reduce to a ½ cup about 20 minutes. Strain and cool.

5. Chop apricots. Combine with wafer crumbs and 1 tb. of pistachios. Stuff half into each pear cavity. Place one pear in each bowl, spoon ¼ cup sauce over pear and sprinkle with pistachios.

4. LEARN FROM EXPERIENCE
Great things with leftovers

*All your experiences are your opportunities
for greater understanding and growth.
Ignore them and you will travel in circles.
Learn from them and you reach the stars.*

This had never happened to Jenny before. She gazed again in astonishment and pleasure at the flower arrangement adorning her dining table. The flowers arrived two days ago, the day after her evening with Serge. The note, still attached to the stem of one bloom, said, "Thank you for a refreshing and delightful evening - to a refreshing and delightful person."

When she called to thank him, Serge invited her to be his guest at the Christmas dinner put on by the corporation he worked for. The telephone conversation lasted for nearly thirty minutes, another first for her. She couldn't wait to tell Nicolas. The thought struck Jenny that in the past, she would have called her mom and told her. Then she would have been disappointed because her mother would have cautioned her and asked a million questions about any potential new man in her life. This time, she would talk to Nicolas first.

"Before you even ask, I have to tell you that I've learned how I can change something that never worked for me in the past," were the first words Jenny uttered, almost before she sat in the chair.

"I'm delighted to hear it," Nicolas replied. "Tell me how you did it, and we will build the recipe for creating success from previous experience."

He listened while Jenny described her successful dinner conversation with Serge, the flowers and note, and subsequent invitation. "I never managed to find someone who would treat me like that or who'd really want to talk to me the way Serge does. The Listening Power recipe really works."

Nicolas cleared his throat as though to say something. She waited, knowing this was a likely moment when she would hear something that would be valuable. She learned that insight came to her when she paid attention to the details.

"Your experiences are the raw material from which you can learn." It was as though Nicolas were talking to himself, his voice was so quiet. Jenny strained to listen. "Most of us simply go through life having experience after experience without ever learning from them. That's fine if life is working well. But if we keep doing things that don't work for us, it's a good idea to stop and do a little reflection on what is happening. So, it seems in this case, Jenny, you have changed the pattern of behavior that did not bring you satisfactory relationships. I want to show you how you can make your previous experiences become your great strengths."

Nicolas picked up a sheet of paper from the small table by his side and handed it to Jenny. She looked at it and studied the five boxes, each of which had a word at the top. It looked like this:

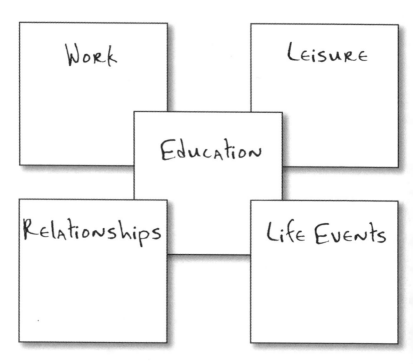

Nicolas continued. "The first part of this recipe, which we can call Learning from Experience, is to put all the ingredients into the pot. In this case, there are five pots. What I'd like you to do, Jenny, is to write down a word or two for as many experiences you can think of and put them into the box that seems the most appropriate. You can go as far back in your life as you like and as recently as the one you just told me about – your dinner with Serge last week. Anything you recall will have significance, even if it seems trivial. The main two things to bear in mind are it must be an experience of your own and it needs to be quite specific. So, for example, don't write down the five years you spent at a certain school, rather put down the particular time you took a test or the conversation you had with a teacher that stayed with you."

Jenny stared at the page, feeling as though her mind had just gone completely blank. She couldn't think of anything. She looked at the first box. Work. Of course, there was the time only a few weeks ago, when she had completely broken down in front of her boss. She wrote down 'break-down.' There must be something more positive. She wrote 'completing the Albany project.' She was especially proud of that. She was getting into her stride now. She wrote five more items down under work and turned to Education. Nicolas had already jogged her memory. She recalled the time she spent an hour with her favorite teacher in fifth grade. They walked around an art gallery, having become separated from the rest of the class. She wrote 'Mrs. Jennings and art gallery.' She wrote four or five items in each box. Five minutes later, Jenny looked up from the page.

"Now that you have put together your basic ingredients, which you can add to at any time, I'd like you to pick one out that you would like to talk about," said Nicolas.

Jenny pondered. "I'll pick one on relationships, since that's what I really want to improve right now. This one: 'breaking up with Peter' is a tough one. I've never wanted to talk about it before; it was so hard. But it was a long time ago now."

"The first stage in this recipe is what we can call 'the story.' Just tell me the story of what happened. I will use Listening Power to help you with that. Then I'll ask you to write down your own summary."

Jenny talked. It was hard at first, bringing tears to her eyes. She knew them as tears of anger and frustration now, not the tears of agony and shame she felt when her first real boyfriend threw her aside when she was eighteen. Then she felt she would never get over it. Now she saw she had wasted a lot of time not getting over it. She noticed Nicolas kept her on track with saying what the experience was instead of getting into the long-term results of her coping with it. He asked her to summarize what she said and write it down on the sheet of paper he handed to her. She made her notes under this heading:

THE STORY
My experience

When she had finished and looked up, Nicolas asked her what she learned from the experience. "This is the second part of your recipe," he offered. "It is the start of your discovery, so you can move this experience from something painful to something of value."

Jenny recalled that pain very clearly. She learned to close down her emotions. She stuffed them, almost literally, by resorting to food. Eating was comfortable, and at first, caused her no shame. She learned to be cautious with men, never believing one would ever commit himself to her. She learned to withhold a large part of who she really was with any other men. She never wanted to be vulnerable again.

Again, Nicolas asked her to summarize what she said by writing it down. This was the heading on the sheet:

DISCOVERY
What I have learned from that experience

"And now," continued Nicolas, almost triumphantly, "I would like to hear how you have demonstrated what you learned. In other words, show me the proof of what you learned as the third stage in this recipe of ours."

Jenny was perplexed. "But I didn't learn anything of much good to me," she began, then realized the effect her reactions had been on the rest of her life. "I guess you could say my weight was the real evidence I ate away my distress. I could never have a decent long-term relationship after that. I would also put myself down until it seemed I could never do anything right."

She was ahead of Nicolas now. "I'll write that down under the next heading." And she did.

PROOF
How I demonstrate what I learned

Jenny was into the swing of things now. Nicolas simply sat back while she went into the next stage – the next part of 'the recipe' as Nicolas would say.

"I think I'm already learning a lot," she said. "I am owning it, too. For years, I blamed Peter for dumping me and attached this to all men. I'm now seeing how much of what went on was my own responsibility. That means I can change it without having to change every man in the world. Or even one. I need to learn how to feel better about myself, how to communicate fully, how to listen better, although I'm doing really well on that, and how not to blame myself when things go wrong. Oh, and how not to resort to addictive eating or anything else if something does go wrong or if someone lets me down."

Jenny wrote under the next heading:

OWNERSHIP
What else I feel I need to learn

Jenny stared for a while at the final heading, her head went blank again after the rush of ideas that just flowed from her. Nicolas came to her rescue. "The last part of this recipe is for you to decide how you are going to learn those things," he prodded. "For example, how are you going to learn to communicate better?"

She stirred herself from her slight paralysis and took up the challenge he just threw at her. Obviously, Nicolas was never going to tell her what to do. "It's started," she acknowledged. "I will continue to talk with Serge the way I did the other evening. I'll remember the contract. In fact, I'll remember and use the whole of Listening Power – and not just with Serge. I'm going to see my mother tomorrow evening and will talk about Serge. If anyone has ever made me feel bad about my relationships it's Mom. It's not that she ever meant to, but it's the way I take it. I will be very clear that I have something to tell her, and I want her to listen to me. I'll tell her how I handled the evening and how great I felt. I am also going to practice that kind of communication with my boss. I know he's seen you, so he'll understand, and it will be easier. We haven't talked about my seeing you yet, but I know he'd love to. I have the feeling we can create a much better working relationship by talking openly about any ideas and concerns we have. I'm sure I could offer him a lot more support if I felt better and more confident about myself."

Jenny became more animated and listed a variety of things she could do to improve things for herself. Nicolas had to help remind her of some of them. She made her final summary under this heading:

GROWTH
What learning opportunities I plan to take up

Back at her house, Jenny read over what she had written and went through it again with a different experience, this time, the one about her teacher and the art gallery. Twenty minutes later, she put down her pen, stretched her neck back, and gave out an enormous sigh that gave vent to the thought filling her head: 'if only I'd seen it before.'

The nine-year-old Jenny, through this special relationship she felt with Mrs. Jennings, had been introduced to art and took this to her heart. As a girl, Jenny threw herself into painting with gusto, partly to please Mrs. Jennings, but increasingly, because she enjoyed it so much. Looking back now, Jenny learned she had a natural creative aptitude but needed the encouragement of someone she respected. She saw that she now used her creative side in small ways, mostly through her cooking, which only seemed to please herself. She understood she needed to learn to paint to please herself. Jenny recalled she told Nicolas she would paint. She had forgotten or pushed it to the back of her mind. She had to take this step. It was a part of her making positive changes in her life. Yes, she'd paint. She would start by enrolling in an art class.

Thinking about that gave her a small lurch of fear. She heard her father telling her that if she wanted to do it, just get on with it. Meanwhile her mother cautioned her not to expect too much. Jenny smiled. They were, after all, both right. She would do it because it was what she wanted and what she knew was important. It was like making the very best of the leftovers of your life.

She had a whole lot of things she was going to do. Art class, talk with her parents in a different way, her boss, and Serge. Jenny smiled. She was tired and rose to get ready for bed. She smiled because she had no impulse to raid the refrigerator.

. . . .

The movie was rated three stars and had the overused 'two thumbs up' claim on its DVD cover. As Serge flicked the remote, he wondered why he hadn't known better. If he listened to his gut instinct instead of his colleague at work, he wouldn't have rented this one. Why didn't he go with his gut more? Why couldn't he trust himself?

Jenny was a case in point. Yes, he was attracted to her. Maybe she was a little overweight, but so was he. They could both do something about that. He knew Jenny was dealing with it better than he was right now. But what really attracted him was how she was. Who she was, really. She wasn't like any of the women he'd known, certainly none of the ones he'd had relationships with.

The problem was they all seemed fine at first. His attraction blinded him to what he later saw as their faults. The common thing was he always felt worthless in the eyes of his girlfriends. Somehow, he always made a mess of things. He didn't understand it because all he wanted was to please them.

Sylvie, for example, was his last real girlfriend, the one he'd been most serious about. They'd lived together for nearly two years. He even thought they were going to get married. Part of his attraction to her was how independent minded she was. She reminded him of his sister. The problem was her independence made her rigid and single minded, so whatever they did had to be her way. If he ever questioned it, she'd go into a rage or simply wouldn't speak to him. Puzzled, he always thought it was his fault that she was unhappy. She reinforced that when she told him he was useless. Nothing he did could satisfy her or make her happy.

He knew now that he was aiming at the impossible, but he didn't know how to change the way he was. Jenny was a million light years away from being Sylvie and different from any other woman he knew. But if he was the same old Serge, would the result be any better? It wasn't fair to her that he still dragged around with him his doubts and memories of those previous bad encounters. He didn't know how to change that. Maybe he could tell Jenny all of this.

Lying awake in bed, he rehearsed what he might say to her. All he received in return was a churning fear in his stomach.

Recipe for Learning from Experience

1. Tell your story

2. Discover what you learned

3. Demonstrate how you use what you learned

4. Take ownership of what you still need to learn

5. Take your learning opportunities for growth

Leftovers
Chicken Lentil Soup

This is a great way to clear out one's refrigerator at the end of the week! Putting a soup together. This soup recipe was created after a harrowing trip through a snowstorm from my parent's place in the country back to their home in the city. The one-hour trip lasted nearly three. Once inside, this quick but delicious soup was made. It has since become a favorite on the table.   *RH*

Recipe designed for 4-6 servings.

1 tb. olive oil	1 tsp. pepper
2 medium onions, diced	1 19-oz. can lentils
2 carrots, medium dice	1 28-oz. can diced tomatoes
2 ribs celery, sliced	1 liter chicken stock
1 small zucchini (½ moons)	3 cups chicken, diced
1 tb. crushed garlic, crushed	¼ cup parsley, minced
1 tb. cumin, ground	1 tb. cornstarch, mixed with
1 tb. Italian seasoning	3 tb. cold water
2 tsp. salt	

Method:

1.   Heat olive oil in large pot. Add onion and sweat (cook on medium heat until translucent).

2.   Add carrots, celery, zucchini, and garlic. Simmer for 5-10 minutes more.

3.   Stir in seasonings, lentils, tomatoes, and chicken stock. If using raw chicken thighs add here. Cover and bring to a boil. Reduce heat and simmer for about 10-15 minutes (or until chicken is cooked).

4.   If using cooked chicken add here (chicken gets tough if cooked too long). Simmer 5 minutes more. Add fresh parsley.

5.   If your soup is thin. Mix cornstarch with water and whisk in to thicken slightly.

6.   Remove from heat and serve with your favorite bread!

5. Gain inner balance
Sweet and sour

All your energy is good.
Your positive energy brings you satisfaction;
your negative energy is your creative potential.
When you learn to transform that potential, you are
ready for more balance and inner peace in your life.

Something was happening to Jenny. She noticed it first as she stepped into her skirt Wednesday morning. It slipped on over her hips more easily than last time she'd worn it. She could put her hand inside the waistband and move it around. She was sure that, last time, she could not have done this. This was despite the quite large meal she and Serge enjoyed at his office party on Saturday. The second thing she noticed was she was smiling.

Jenny never did well on diets. She was not on a diet now. The difference was, since she started to feel a whole lot better about herself, she no longer snacked on the sweet, and often fatty, extras that had become part of her everyday habits.

As she dressed for work, Jenny reflected on the previous few days, feeling almost light-headed at the torrent of things that happened. First, and most thrilling of all, was her growing relationship with Serge. With him, she felt special, attractive, and enlivened. Even more important, she felt like that most of the time now. Their conversation, their connection, and their shared values had turned into a physical attraction she had not expected. Jenny hugged herself as she basked again in the memory of the Sunday afternoon and evening she spent with Serge.

While the other things that happened paled by comparison, Jenny knew they were vital steps in her continued transformation. She signed up for a painting class at the local college to start in the New Year. She talked with her mother, and not only found her supportive and understanding, but discovered things about her she had never known. Her conversations with her father were not quite as amazing, but she was able to talk with him on a level where she at least felt adult and not his little girl.

This evening was her fifth session with Nicolas. She looked forward to it. But first, she looked forward to a day at work, despite feeling a flutter of anxiety. This was the other thing that happened. She spoke with her boss, suggesting she take the lead on a new project. To her surprise, he agreed, on the understanding that Jenny would come to him any time she was uncertain. She would report to him on a regular basis. Today was the day he would hand over the files. Jenny experienced a new confidence. After all, hadn't she recognized her abilities when she recounted the success of the Albany project? It might have been a different employer and nearly five years ago, but she proved her worth then and could do it again now. The Learning from Experience story she wrote gave Jenny the confidence she needed to move ahead in her career.

Sitting in the now familiar chair, she recounted to Nicolas some of her progress. When she finished, Nicolas asked, "Where do you want to take things now?"

Jenny reflected on this, aware that she was a little taken aback. Nicolas didn't congratulate her or appear pleased that she had done so well. It was as though he was her father, always pushing her to be better or do more. A surge of resentment rose up in her. She then realized she was glaring at Nicolas. That's when a light went on in her head. She gave away her sense of achievement and her own power when someone, almost always a man in some authority over her, failed to show admiration for her. Jenny smiled. "I think I want to look at how I give away my power," she said. "I want to know what I need to do to remember I'm okay."

Nicolas reached down to a sheaf of paper at his side. "I think you know, Jenny, that this is all about how you can empower yourself more. Here's something you can do. I'll take you through it. It's a way for you to see where your emotional balance is right now and how you can make the changes that are beneficial for you. It's called the Lifescale. There are ten questions in it. Five of them look at the things that satisfy you in your life or the things that bring you your positive emotional energy. Five look at the things that frustrate you or give you negative emotional energy. I'd like you to give each of the questions a score, from zero to twenty, depending on how you feel at this point in your life. I can't interpret the scores. I wouldn't even if I could. But you will, and I'll help you to do that."

With that, Nicolas passed her the Lifescale.

Lifescale

NAME . . . .   **DATE** . . . .

Score each question on a scale 0 – 20

1. How much PLEASURE do I get from life? .   □

2. How much PAIN do I feel I have? · · · · · · · · · · · □

3. How much PURPOSE do I have in my life? . . □

4. How much do PROBLEMS weigh me down? . . . . □

5. How much do I feel I'm in the right PLACE? . □

6. How much PREJUDICE do I feel against me? . . . . □

7. How much POWER do I feel I have? . . . . . . □

8. How much POVERTY do I feel I have? . . . . □

9. How much PEACE of mind do I feel? . . . . . □

10. How much PRESSURE do I feel is on me? . . . . □

TOTAL SCORES . . . .   □ □

Jenny looked it over quickly and began filling in the scores. As she did so, she concentrated on the experiences and feelings that each question brought to her. Deciding on a score was sometimes hard. She forced herself to attach the score that came more from her feelings than her trying to figure out all the possibilities. This is what her Lifescale looked like after she filled in her scores:

Lifescale

NAME: Jenny Cunningham   **DATE:** December 21, 2005

Score each question on a scale 0 – 20

1. How much PLEASURE do I get from life? . . `15`

2. How much PAIN do I feel I have? · · · · · · · · · · · · · `8`

3. How much PURPOSE do I have in my life? . . `8`

4. How much do PROBLEMS weigh me down? . . . . `10`

5. How much do I feel I'm in the right PLACE? . `12`

6. How much PREJUDICE do I feel against me? . . . . `5`

7. How much POWER do I feel I have? . . . . . . `12`

8. How much POVERTY do I feel I have? . . . . `6`

9. How much PEACE of mind do I feel? . . . . . `12`

10. How much PRESSURE do I feel is on me? . . . . `10`

TOTAL SCORES . . . . `59`   `39`

Jenny wasn't sure what her scores should look like. She felt a vague sense of disappointment at what seemed to be some low scores, especially for how much purpose she had, while some of the others, like how much pain she felt and the ones about pressure and problems seemed too high for comfort. On the other hand, these scores were a lot better than they would have been a few weeks ago. Then, she'd have put hardly anything for how much pleasure she had and would maybe score 20 for how much pain she felt. She was grateful Nicolas hadn't shown her the Lifescale then. She looked up.

"This is the third recipe in your search for inner peace, Jenny," said Nicolas. "The ingredients are the ten questions with the scores you gave them. The important part of the mix comes next. Take a look at the first one. I see you've put 15 out of 20 for how much pleasure you feel. Tell me what this 15 means to you."

Jenny stared at the 15 in front of her. What did it mean to her? Once again, she thought how much it had changed over the past few weeks, since she met Serge and became more comfortable with herself. And yet, was this 15 just dependent on someone else or how she felt right now?

"I think this 15 means that, underneath everything, I am basically a happy person," she responded at last. "I do feel great about my relationship with Serge. I don't even mind what happens with it right now. I am just having so much fun with him. I am getting more pleasure from my work. I feel free to be who I am with my friends and even with my parents."

Nicolas tilted his head. "And what would it be like if you had 20? What would the other five be for you?"

This was unexpected, although Jenny was used to the unexpected questions Nicolas asked. They were the ones that stopped her in her tracks and often shone a brighter light into the recesses of her mind. This was no exception. It was just as though the light shone on the thoughts she had earlier. She tried to grasp the idea floating around. Talking out loud would help her make sense of it.

"The other five would be if I knew deep inside me I would feel pleasure, whatever was going on around me. Even though I have lots of pleasure right now, I can't have more until I have that deep inner feeling that I'm just fine. Does that make sense?"

"Does it make sense to you?"

That was a typical Nicolas response, she thought. She knew it was the only thing that mattered. Yes, it made sense to her. It made so much sense she gave a broad grin. Something certainly was happening.

Nicolas gave one of his succinct and accurate summaries of what she said and asked her to write down her own summary on the next page in answer to the first question. It was:

What does my score for PLEASURE mean to me?

This is what Jenny wrote:

My 15 for pleasure means I am having a lot of fun in my life right now, enjoying my relationship with Serge, having an easier time relating to my parents and at work, and feeling more comfortable with myself. It's not more than 15 because I still want to know I can feel this pleasure without depending on others or circumstances outside of me.

She read back what she wrote to Nicolas, who invited her to explain the meaning of the eight she gave to the next question: How much pain do I feel in my life? She spoke about what the eight meant to her. Again, she had some insights. Finally, she wrote down her summary underneath the second question:

What does my score for PAIN mean to me?

My eight for pain means I am holding onto some of the bad feelings I have had for so long, that caused me to lock up emotionally. I still have doubts about whether my good feelings are going to last or whether they are real.

Jenny was getting into the swing of this. Time was running out in the hour she had with Nicolas, but now she wanted to get through this Lifescale as soon as possible. She didn't want to wait until next time, which was going to be two weeks because of the Christmas break.

She told Nicolas.

"You can go through them yourself now that you've started," he offered. " We can speak on the phone or via e-mail. I'd like to go through the summaries at the end, after you have looked at each of the questions."

The next day was her last-minute shopping night with a couple of her girlfriends. Jenny decided to spend the following evening, Friday, with her Lifescale. Serge suggested meeting her after work on Friday, but she opted to skip that and spend Saturday evening, which was Christmas Eve, with him as they had already planned. He sounded a little put out, but she chose to ignore it. She wasn't going to let other people's insecurities affect her any more. In any case, there was this big buildup for the celebrations at home on Sunday, when Serge would be introduced to the family. She needed to have this little bit of time for herself.

It was easier and harder to answer the questions on her own. Easier, because she could just write down her response; harder, because after she wrote her response, she saw things that were underneath the obvious, as though she were hearing those difficult questions that Nicolas asked her. Eventually, she was happy with what she wrote. It was nearly 9:00 p.m. on Friday. She didn't want to disturb Nicolas at that time, but she decided to e-mail him with her summaries. He could respond in his own time, and if it were after Christmas, she'd just have to wait. This is what she sent:

What does my score for PURPOSE mean to me?

My eight for purpose means I am unsure about it. I think I'm here for a reason and have a lot to offer. I want to be more fulfilled. That means I want to be more creative. I want to be a joy to others. So I am not halfway there yet.

What does my score for PROBLEMS mean to me?

I gave 10 for this. I realize the only problems are the ones I give myself, so this is high. I have stopped myself from doing things and have made myself miserable. I am moving, but I still have too many doubts that hold me back. On the other hand, I am going in the right direction. This would have been at least 15 before.

What does my score for PLACE mean to me?

The 12 I feel for place is mostly about where I live. I'm happy with my home and living near my family in this great town. Some of it is about feeling that I am going in the right direction with being who I am. There seems a long way to go before I am totally comfortable with just being me. If this were 20, I'd be happily married and feeling great about life.

What does my score for PREJUDICE mean to me?

I don't feel any prejudice against me, but I put five because I let others put me down. That means my dad or other men in authority, but they don't even mean to do it. It's how I react. I'm prejudiced against myself when I don't believe in me.

What does my score for POWER mean to me?

I'm getting there! Twelve is a lot higher than it was. I feel powerful when I stand up for myself and ask for what I want. I am more powerful when I listen to myself, which I am doing a lot more now. It's not more than 12 because I still doubt whether I can keep this up. Will my job work out okay? Will I frighten Serge off if I'm too pushy?

What does my score for POVERTY mean to me?

I don't feel poor in money terms. I do have to watch what I spend, but I am fairly careful and earn a good salary. The six is mostly for what I lack personally. Something inside that wants to come out. I think it's my creative side.

What does my score for PEACE mean to me?

This feels a lot better than before. Twelve means I am a lot more at peace with myself. The rest is still that uncertainty. Is it real? Can I sustain this? If I had 20, it would mean I'd feel great no matter what. That doesn't seem possible yet.

What does my score for PRESSURE mean to me?

I feel pressure mostly from me. It used to be that I felt the pressure from my boss or my dad. Now it's 10, and most of it is mine. I think I have to hang on to it until I figure out why I need it.

The next morning was one of those clear blue-sky days. Light snow had fallen overnight, giving everything a crisp, clean, silent atmosphere. Jenny had a busy day ahead of her. She had presents to wrap and a meal to make for this evening. Serge was coming, and she planned something different.

She checked her computer around midday. To her surprise, she found a reply from Nicolas. Did he plan to work over the weekend, even at Christmas? Well, not quite. The reply was brief.

"Thanks for sending this, Jenny. Give me a call on Wednesday, and we'll go through the rest before you come to see me the following week. Meanwhile, have a wonderful holiday break. Nicolas."

That evening was the most unusual and most satisfying of Christmas Eves that Jenny had experienced since she was a small child. Serge told her how much he loved oriental food and especially the contrasts of flavors.

When Jenny saw the Lifescale, it struck her that this was the ideal meal to cook up. The Lifescale was the sweet and sour side of life. You didn't want too much or too little of either, but together, in the right balance, they were perfect. The trick was to get the right balance.

"Great meal," Serge sighed as he chased a stray grain of rice around with his chopsticks. "You're a wonderful cook Jenny."

"Well thank you," she replied, blushing slightly. "You remember the first time you came for a meal and we talked, or rather, we listened to each other? I was wondering if we could do that again but a little differently."

"Sure. What do you have in mind?"

"I have done this thing called a Lifescale. I haven't finished it yet, but I'd like to tell you about it and what I have found out about myself. I'd like you to listen to the answers I gave to some amazing questions. If you want to, you could say how you might answer the same questions, and I'll just listen to you. I thought we'd find out more about each other that way."

Serge shuffled in his chair. Not much, but enough for Jenny to notice his discomfort. He cleared his throat. "Well, sure," he said.

"I don't want to force you into anything you don't feel comfortable about." Jenny suddenly felt uneasy. She wanted to show empathy for Serge, but she noticed the anxiety rise in her. Was she going too far, getting pushy, scaring Serge away?

"It's fine, Jenny." Serge was smiling at her. "Please tell me about it. I must be honest; you do give me a hard time sometimes. I'm not used to talking about this kind of stuff. I suppose it kind of scares me. But I have to admit when we do talk like this, I feel pretty good about it. It's so different. You're so different." He seemed as though he wanted to say more, but the words tailed off at the end. His looked down at his empty bowl as if he might find some missing scrap that could help him out.

Jenny talked about her Lifescale answers. From the start, when he heard his name in the very first response, Serge wanted to ask her more. When she read out the piece about being married, he was quiet, as though he withdrew from her. When she spoke about not frightening him off by being too pushy, he denied this would happen. She had to remind him she just wanted him to listen to her. "Or is that being too pushy?" she asked.

"I think you're amazing, doing this stuff," was his response. "It's too much for me right now. I may want to do this later, when I've let it sink in a bit more. You're right, though. I've found out more about you in this short time than I think I know about anyone in the world. It seems like you've trusted me with something really precious. I wish I could feel ready to do the same, but I'm sure I will soon."

Jenny's heart leapt when Serge began speaking and dropped through to her knees by the time he finished. She knew it. She frightened him off. He was too gentle a man to drop her just like that, but he surely would.

It was late. Serge helped her clear up, told her how much he looked forward to spending Christmas day with her family, kissed her warmly, rather than passionately, and left.

The following week, she called Nicolas. "Yes, Christmas was good," she answered in response to his enquiry. "Serge got on really well with Mom and Dad. I just wish I felt better about it. I still have this sense of not being a part of what's going on. I made a big mistake. I asked Serge to do the Lifescale, and he backed off."

"Sounds as though that was a little premature, Jenny. Let's complete your own and that may help you to make sense of some of your feelings and actions. First I want you to look at the five questions that deal with your positive emotional side. Those are the questions about pleasure, purpose, place, power, and peace of mind. The total you have for those questions are 59, right? That 59 out of a possible 100 total represents your satisfactions. Now, looking over what you said about those questions, tell me what your satisfactions mean to you."

Jenny stared at her previous notes. With a little gentle prompting from Nicolas, she wrote down her summary, then read it out loud.

"I am getting more comfortable with who I am but carry doubts about sustaining the progress I'm making and if I can let go of my dependence on others making me feel good."

"Good," said Nicolas. "Now do the same for the other questions, the negative emotional side, or your frustrations score, which added up to 39."

Jenny could do this herself.

"I'm holding on to old doubts about myself. That holds me back from having healthy relationships and from letting out my creative side."

"Excellent," said Nicolas. (Jenny couldn't recall him using that word before.) And now, put the two together, and make a summary of what your Lifescale means to you right now."

They talked about this for a few minutes. Nicolas asked Jenny to notice the connections and the essence of what she was saying. Up to this point, she found this to be a bit laborious. As she looked at her two summaries, Jenny saw something with blinding clarity. It was obvious, and yet, she had not understood. She couldn't wait to write it down.

"I really am moving," she read back to Nicolas. "Of course, I have doubts, but what's harder to face now is I am really making progress. I fear having a good relationship with myself because of what I absorbed from others in the past. I don't need to hold on any more."

Jenny didn't know where that came from, but she could hardly contain her excitement. "I feel like I've suddenly grown up, and I don't have to hang on to the fears about whether or not I'm good enough. It's my choice now."

"That's powerful stuff Jenny," said Nicolas. "Finally, I want you to write down one more thing. What action are you going to take?"

Jenny hardly had to think about it.

"Step through the doubts and be me. Whatever happens, I have to do what is real and important for me. I will say what's right. I will not let my fears stop me from being who I am."

Jenny paused after reading it back to Nicolas. "Is that specific enough?" she asked him. She heard Nicolas smile at the other end of the phone.

Meanwhile, Serge was doing some thinking of his own.

. . . .

New Year with the family was always a joyous occasion. Odd then, how Serge did not seem joyous. Maybe he had imported the feeling of joyousness from his sister, parents, and more recently, his nephew and nieces, and it wasn't really his to feel. This year, more than any other, he felt confused.

He was confused about his real feelings. He was confused about who he was and who he was supposed to be. They seemed to be two different things, which was confusing. He was confused about Jenny.

He enjoyed her company, really enjoyed being with her, and always looked forward to seeing her. He loved the way she shared her thoughts with him. More than anything, it showed she trusted him. That was something new in his life. But he increasingly felt a sense of pressure when he was with her. That was nothing new. He felt the pressure now, in the midst of his family, in the midst of the happy sharing of stories and celebration of their annual reunion.

If only he could shake this off. If only he could trust himself in the same way that Jenny seemed to trust him. If only he deserved to be trusted. But what was there not to trust? He looked around at the faces of his family. He wanted to be a part of them, and yet, he felt he didn't really belong. What was wrong with him?

In his room, his old room that was always ready for him, even though he might not be there for a year, Serge took the Lifescale from his suitcase. Jenny had given him one to 'try out.' Maybe he could give it a whirl.

Lifescale

NAME: Serge Zurowski   **DATE:** January 1, 2006

Score each question on a scale 0 – 20

1. How much PLEASURE do I get from life? . . | 9 |

2. How much PAIN do I feel I have? · · · · · · · · · · · | 9 |

3. How much PURPOSE do I have in my life? . . | 6 |

4. How much do PROBLEMS weigh me down? . . . . . . · | 12 |

5. How much do I feel I'm in the right PLACE? . | 6 |

6. How much PREJUDICE do I feel against me? . . . . . . · | 7 |

7. How much POWER do I feel I have? . . . . . | 10 |

8. How much POVERTY do I feel I have? . . . . | 3 |

9. How much PEACE of mind do I feel? . . . . . | 6 |

10. How much PRESSURE do I feel is on me? . . . . | 15 |

TOTAL SCORES . . . . | 37 | | 46 |

Jenny had wanted him to look at his Lifescale with her. He looked at his scores and saw why he didn't want to. He felt ashamed. He was especially ashamed of his low score for purpose. When he looked at all the scores, it seemed as though he was complaining when there was nothing to complain about. What was this pain he felt? Nothing physical.

And the problems, what were they? As for pressure, nobody was putting any pressure on him except himself. He didn't even know what the pressure was.

Something dawned on him.

Serge looked at the rest of the Lifescale and wrote down the answers to the questions. As he wrote, the emerging notion that he had glimpsed became clearer and clearer. The only problem was the way he saw things. He saw things in two distinct ways. One was through the eyes of his sister, the way he thought he should be. The other was in his way and that was never good enough. No one in his family had ever said that, but he invented his own story about not being as good as his twin. No wonder he was confused. No wonder he didn't feel much sense of purpose. No wonder he put so much pressure on himself.

Now what was he supposed to do?

Recipe for Inner Balance

1. Answer the 10 Lifescale questions
2. Say what each means to you
3. Make the connections in your answers
4. Decide what you want to change
5. Keep practicing, with someone else listening.

Sweet and Sour

Sweet and Sour Jumbo Shrimp

Juicy succulent jumbo shrimp are lightly coated and tossed with vegetables in a homemade sweet and sour sauce.   RH

This recipe is designed for 4 people.

Sweet and Sour Sauce

1 orange peel roughly cut
1 clove garlic, crushed
2 tb. canola oil
½ cup red wine vinegar
½ cup rice wine vinegar
1½ cups pineapple juice
½ cup dark sugar
½ cup tomato ketchup
2 tb. soy sauce
2 tb. sesame oil
2 tb. cornstarch dissolved in 3/4 cup cold water

Method:

1.   Saute the orange peel and garlic in the oil for 5 minutes.

2.   Add all of the remaining ingredients except for the cornstarch, bring to a boil. Reduce heat and simmer for 30 minutes.

3.   Add the cornstarch and return to a boil. Strain and adjust the seasoning to taste by using vinegar, sugar, or water.

4.   Set aside while preparing jumbo shrimp.

Jumbo Shrimp

16 medium large shrimp
2 tb. canola oil
1 cup flour
1 tb. dried parsley
½ tsp. salt
½ tsp. pepper

Method:

1.   Peel shrimp and devein.

2.   Combine flour, parsley, salt, and pepper. Toss shrimp in flour
      mixture and place in pan.

3.   Cook shrimp until brown all over, about 5 minutes.

4.   Remove from pan, and add vegetables.

Vegetables

---

1 carrot, peeled and cut on the bias (Asian style)
3 green onions, cut 2 inches long
½ cup diced pineapple
½ green or yellow pepper, cubed
½ cup cherry tomatoes, cut in half

Method:

1.   Add vegetables and sauté until bright in color.

2.   Add jumbo shrimp and sauce, heat gently for 5 minutes or
        until heated through.

Serve over a wonderful and fragrant bed of scrumptious rice such as
basmati or jasmine.

Enjoy!

6. Meet your authentic self
Food for the kid in you

Play. Your inner wisdom comes from your child self. As you reconnect, you will travel through time and arrive at the place of your dreams.

$\mathcal{S}$erge sat at a table at the back of the café where he often ate alone at some time after one o'clock. He preferred his own company during the week, instead of the noontime hustle to grab a bite with some of his work colleagues. A book or a newspaper was the kind of company he liked.

Today, Serge had nothing to read. Instead, he pulled out a tablet of paper and a pen. He scribbled the words that flowed from him while he waited for his soup and sandwich to arrive.

The family reunion had been an eye-opener once he decided to discover how he became the man he was. He spent the last full day listening and observing. He took in information he already knew. He heard it in a new and enlightened way, revealing more about his family and him than he cared to register.

Serge wrote fragments as they came to him.

Dad sat smiling at everyone, saying very little except to agree with Mom and Laurette. I noticed how much it annoyed me. Then I saw that's exactly what I do. Mom constantly tells the girls how well they are doing and reminds Gary he hasn't washed his hands. I recall that's just how it was for me. Laurette suggested we play charades, and I suddenly felt shy. Of course, we play charades, even though Gary and Sarah resist. It seems only Justine really wants to, so she and Laurette get their way. That's just how it was when we were kids. I'd feel out of place. Looking at Dad, Gary, Justine, and their dad, I realized I'm not the only one. Mom probably felt out of it too but never showed anything except how enthusiastic she was about almost everything. Maybe even Justine and her mom didn't feel part of things and were putting on a face. Is that what we all did? Put a mask on, pretending to be someone we thought we're supposed to be? If that's so, did anyone else realize it? If I'm the only one who realized we were all wearing masks, that's another reason for me to feel left out. No wonder I'm confused! At least I'm getting clearer about my confusion.

Serge took a spoon of soup. It was only just warm.

. . . .

"Our fourth life recipe is what I call the Time Capsule." Nicolas leaned back in his chair and gave Jenny a thoughtful look. "I'd like you to tell me about something that's been going on for you in the past week;

something that provides an example of one of the things that has caused you concern."

"You mean like feeling guilty or not being able to make good relationships?" asked Jenny.

"Exactly so but a specific event that just happened."

"Well, I could talk about the conversation I had with Serge yesterday. That seemed to get me into a pattern I don't feel good about. I asked him if he still felt like I was putting too much pressure on him. He told me he did feel pressure but that it had nothing to do with me. When I asked him what he meant, he said I reminded him of his sister. I hardly heard anything else he said after that because I was so shocked. I mean the last person I want to be is his sister. I don't know her, but if he sees me that way then what chance do we have? I always thought no man would ever love me." Jenny began to cry softly. Between sniffles, she continued. "I wasn't able to listen to him properly. Even when he told me he didn't mean what I thought, it just seemed to get worse."

Nicolas repeated back to Jenny what she'd said. As she heard it, it suddenly seemed less dramatic than her experience of it. She wondered why she made such a big deal out of it. Then Nicolas asked her a strange question.

"Tell me about an early experience, one that you can recall from your childhood. I'd like you to relate it to me as though it were happening now. Tell me how old you are, what you see around you, who's there, if anyone, where you are, and what's going on."

Jenny stopped sniffing. Her body relaxed, but her mind whirled back into her childhood. Memories, some of them very vague, floated in and out like a slide show of old photographs. One slide stood out, settled in her mind, and the picture beckoned to her.

"I must be about four or five," she began slowly. "I'm with lots of other kids. We're having a party." Jenny's eyes widened. "Oh, I remember now. It's my birthday. I must have been five. It was my party."

Nicolas interjected. "Stay in the present Jenny. I want you to be that birthday girl telling me what's happening."

"It's my party. I'm wearing a white and pink frock. My mother is bringing in the birthday cake. Everyone is cheering. I feel so proud and happy because this is for me, all this celebration. Then the cake is cut up and everyone has a piece. Suddenly, I feel very sad. One girl – I can't remember her name, but she's quite a fat little girl – grabs a second slice of cake. I get really angry with her. We have a fight before my mom steps in. That's all I remember."

There was a silence as Jenny's mind swirled with fragments of the memory she had just rekindled. Nicolas patiently waited for her to come back to the present.

He began. "I'd like you, as Jenny now, to transport yourself back into that party, so you and five-year-old Jenny can see each other. What do you have to say to little Jenny?"

Another silence fell, as Jenny nudged towards an insight she felt was already changing something deep within her. Her chest felt tight. It was difficult for her to breathe. Tears sprang to her eyes. She knew the words but none came out. Nicolas gently told her to take her time, the exact encouragement she needed to begin.

"I can see you're sad and angry," she spoke, in a voice just above a whisper. "It's your birthday, and I just want you to be happy." This wasn't exactly what Jenny wanted to say, but it was a start. Too many ideas were competing in her head. She paused, looked at Nicolas, who sat completely still, waiting, it seemed, for her to sort out her thoughts. She relaxed, knowing it would come out just right.

"You see," she continued, "the cake is a celebration, and everyone wants to share it. They are sharing your cake. That little fat girl, maybe she is a bit unhappy herself and feels she needs another slice."

Nicolas crossed his legs. "When little Jenny hears that, how is she feeling? What does she say back to you?"

Jenny felt as though she were wearing that party dress again. "She feels confused. Why does she have to share with the others? Why does that girl need more? Now she feels ashamed. She felt ashamed then, I remember now. She says to me: 'It doesn't feel like my party anymore. It doesn't feel like I deserve to be happy.' Now I just want to pick her up and hold her and tell her she's fine, that she deserves every bit of happiness."

"Can you do that, Jenny?"

"Yes I can." And Jenny's tears flowed.

When he deemed she was ready, Nicolas invited her to take the next stage in the Time Capsule. "Leave the party behind you, Jenny. Now I want little Jenny to come into the present with you and tell you what she sees as you get upset with Serge when he says you remind him of his sister."

This surprised her. She had begun to make a vague, although powerful, connection with the fat little girl at her party, but she had not considered any connection with Serge and the conversation she talked about earlier. Her mind spun again. She was more conscious of the emotional clarity that was starting to emerge.

"Little Jennifer tells me she wants me to be happy. That means I'd better understand about sharing. She tells me Serge didn't mean to take anything away from me. He loves his sister. He was just telling me he felt pressure from her, which is his problem. He wanted to share that with me. I thought he was taking something away, that I didn't deserve his love. The other thing is," Jenny looked over at Nicolas, "I have always had that fat girl in my mind for years and somehow identified with her. That extra piece of cake had a huge affect on me."

"Anything else little Jennifer wants to say to you?"

She thought for a moment. "Yes, she tells me I'm doing okay now as long as I remember she's the five-year-old girl, and I'm twenty-eight. When Serge talked to me, I felt like I was five all over again. When I raided the refrigerator, I was that little girl needing more cake every time. Oh my!"

"Now Jenny, I want you to get back in this Time Capsule you have been traveling in. This time take yourself into the future. It's one year from now. Tell me what's happening at this moment in your life."

The journey she started weeks ago with Nicolas was moving fast now. Jenny felt breathless.

"I'm with friends," she said. "We're laughing, telling each other about the things going on in our lives. I feel happy and content."

"So now I'd like you to visit Jenny in the future, feeling happy and content and sharing that with her friends. What do you want to say to her or ask her?"

"I'm glad for you. You deserve it. Do you think I can get there?"

"What does she answer?" enquired Nicolas.

"You're on the right track. Keep doing what you're doing now, and you'll be exactly here. I'm proud of you for coming such a long way already."

Jenny's eyes welled up again, but she was smiling.

Later that evening, Serge took Jenny to his favorite dessert café. They ordered an ice cream between the two of them. Jenny was delighted that she suggested they share, and even more so when Serge agreed.

Before it arrived, they were deep into conversation, the topic of which was the observations Serge had made about his family. Jenny held back her own desire to talk about her new insights, even though she was bursting. She remembered her Listening Power and set a contract with Serge that she'd listen to him first. She wanted some time to talk too.

But Serge was downcast, talking in a low tone about how everyone seemed to be playing games instead of being real.

He felt unable to do anything to change his feelings of being an outsider.

Jenny tried to reassure him. "You're real to me Serge," she told him, putting her hand on his arm. "I want to be with you, so you don't need to feel like an outsider."

He pulled away. "I don't want your sympathy, Jenny. I have to figure this out myself."

The chasm grew between them. Jenny saw he was right. Serge had to figure it out himself, just as she was doing it for herself. Her concern was seen as pressure, which was his issue, not hers. She would not be drawn into her own cycle of feeling undeserving.

The ice cream turned soft, melting on its dish. Serge dipped into his self-wallowing, while Jenny dipped her spoon into the treat he seemed determined to miss.

Recipe for Finding Your Authentic Self

1. Look at a pattern you want to change
2. Explore the last time it showed itself
3. Look at an early experience
4. Talk with your child in that experience
5. Look at you in the future
6. Have a dialogue with your future self.

Food for the kid in you

Vanilla Bean Ice Cream with Chocolate Drizzle

During my school year with the culinary arts, I entered a four-course meal in a prestigious cooking competition. I won first place for this vanilla bean ice cream. The prize was a weekend trip to Jasper, Alberta. This recipe has been designed for 6-8 servings. RH

2 cups 32 percent cream
1 cup whole milk
3/4 cup sugar
1/8 tsp. salt
3 vanilla beans, split lengthwise
2 large eggs

Method:

1. Combine cream, milk, sugar, and salt in a heavy saucepan. Scrape seeds from vanilla beans with tip of a knife into cream mixture, then drop in pods. Heat mixture just to a boil.

2. Whisk eggs in a large bowl, then add hot cream mixture in a slow stream, whisking. Pour mixture into saucepan and cook over medium, low heat, stirring constantly, until slightly thickened. (Thermometer registers 170°F.) Do not boil!

3. Pour custard through a fine sieve into a clean metal bowl and cool. Stir occasionally. Chill, cover until cold, about 3 hours.

4. Freeze custard in an ice cream maker or in a freezer friendly container. If not making in an ice cream maker, remove frozen ice cream from freezer, blend in blender and refreeze.

Chocolate drizzle

5 tb. sugar
¼ cup light corn syrup
¼ cup heavy cream
1 cup good quality chocolate, broken into small pieces
1 tb. vanilla extract
1 tb. Grand Marnier
1 tb. water

Method:
1.   Place sugar, syrup, cream, and chocolate into a heavy saucepan, over medium heat. Stir continuously until the chocolate is melted.

2.   Add the remaining ingredients, bring to a boil, and set aside until ready to serve.

7. Dialogue with others
Dinner parties made easy

Each of us is unique. All of us are connected.
When we share in that spirit of understanding,
we can travel together.

Rick entered the room holding a coffee in one hand, his cell phone in the other. A large folder was tucked under his arm. As he juggled to set them down on the glass-topped table, while pushing the door closed with his elbow, the other members of the team looked at each other in varying expressions of bewilderment, impatience, humor, and resignation. The weekly meeting, which was cancelled more often than not, or at best started late, was about to begin.

Serge liked Rick's easygoing nature but cringed at his disorganization, reflecting to himself that the two were probably connected.

"Sorry," Rick bellowed to the room in general. "Just had to sort out an emergency with Human Resources."

Heads nodded lethargically. Serge heard the word 'emergency' too many times from Rick to believe it was anything more significant than an enquiry about a new employee.

"Now, let's see. What do we have?" Rick started the meeting.

Serge watched and listened. He was well prepared for his item on the agenda, so concentrated on what went on between the people sitting around the table. It was just like observing his family. He saw the masks they wore. These masks were mostly related to the role each person had in the department and the character and personality each tried to portray. He looked around the room.

Rick, ruffling though his papers, sat at the head of the table. The impression of disorganization disappeared when, whatever the agenda item and whoever was presenting it, Rick suddenly became the expert. Serge noticed how one by one, after being invited to present his or her item, each team member gradually became silent, sullen, or argumentative when Rick intervened after only a few moments and took over the conversation.

Elsie, on Rick's left, nodded a lot at Rick's comments, sometimes injecting what appeared to be her own view, which always agreed with Rick's.

Next to her, Grant sat with his hand to his forehead, looking down at the table, doodling on his scratch pad. He said nothing unless Rick asked him to, apart from the occasional neutral grunt.

Ray was the humorist of the group, constantly making little jokes or laughing at any *double-entendre*, sometimes, Serge felt, quite inappropriately. When he gave his report and Rick interrupted him, Ray became angry, raising his voice and interrupting Rick in return. "This is what I'm paid to do. I know how to do it," he exclaimed. "If you don't trust me to get it right, it's a waste of time. But you're the boss. If you want it your way, I'll do it." He laughed, looking around the room in triumph. Serge realized this scenario played out almost every time.

Over the next hour, Serge discovered nobody listened to anyone else or dealt with the discontent and frustration that clearly existed. He saw decisions that were bad, vague, deferred, or simply avoided. He wondered how much this would cost the company when things went wrong or had to be repeated.

When his turn came, Serge looked up at Rick. "Before I start," he said, "I have a request. I'd like to make my brief report without being interrupted."

"That's a laugh," quipped Ray.

"No, I'm serious. I'd appreciate your help, Ray."

Ray sat back in his chair, his mouth opened as if about to make a comment, then closed as he thought better of it or he could think of nothing to say. Rick raised his eyebrows and pursed his lips as though in a conscious effort to keep them together.

"I have three main points," continued Serge, "and there's one decision to be made. I'll give the options as I see them, with my preference. When I've finished, I'd like to invite ideas and suggestions from anyone in the team. I think everyone might have something to offer."

It was a risk, and Serge felt a tightening of his chest. Seven pairs of eyes met his as he looked around the table. Surprised, even shocked, expressions came back to him.

"Go ahead Serge," offered Rick.

Serge gave his report without interruption. It didn't go quite as he hoped after that, and as he and Jenny had discussed, but it was a whole lot better than the rest of the meeting had been.

As they broke up, nobody mentioned anything about it. Serge felt like he was being avoided, shunned. He went back to his office and closed the door.

. . . .

Jenny took the scones out of the oven. They would still be warm when people arrived. It was an inspiration to invite six of her girlfriends to dinner. Now she felt nervous.

She'd discussed this with Nicolas last week. "How do I get a group of friends to listen to each other?" she asked. "Whenever we get together, everyone babbles away at the same time. We have fun, but I never seem to get to know anybody."

Nicolas took her through his fifth recipe, the Group Dialogue. "It's like Listening Power, except you apply it in a group. I've used it with boardroom executives and family groups. It always works. There are seven stages. I'll tell you what they are. Ask your friends to go along with it. I'm sure you will all find it an interesting and enlightening experience."

As Jenny put the finishing touches to her table, the doorbell rang. The first of her guests arrived. Soon, they were all there: Alex, Marge, Fran, Linda, Jolene, and Maya, all admiring Jenny's décor and munching her scones.

It was what Jenny described as a rustic meal. The friends dipped into their stew with gusto. While they finished off the crumbs of the apple ginger pies, Jenny served herbal tea from a large pot. "Now girls," she said. "I have something a little different I'd like us to do. You know how we just have conversations, and it goes from one thing to another and one person to another? Well, I have discovered a way of having conversation that changes how we listen."

A wave of laughter - Jenny thought it sounded like an undercurrent of embarrassment - swept around the table.

"You mean we have to listen as well as talk?" joked Fran. "Not sure I can cope with that after such a fun time."

"How does it work?" asked Jolene, her head tilted at Jenny in obvious interest.

"I'll take us through it if you like. We can try it once. If it works and we enjoy it, we can do it again," said Jenny. "I haven't tried it myself yet, so you'll be my first experiment. To tell the truth, I'm a little scared. I don't want to lose the few friends I have. You're it, you know. But I do trust you all, which is why I asked you."

"Well, I'm willing to have a go," declared Alex, and all the others nodded and murmured their assent.

Jenny took a deep breath. "Here's what we do then."

Two hours later, the last person left. Everything was cleared away. Her friends had insisted they help with the dishes. The genuine laughter that accompanied the clattering of plates still reverberated in Jenny's ears.

Snuggling down in her bed, she flushed with satisfaction as she relived the warmth of the hugs and comments that each of her girlfriends gave at the door. "The best evening we ever had," said Maya. Everyone else agreed.

Jenny had gone over the Group Dialogue process. Alex offered to speak first. It was difficult to stick to the 'rules' initially, but Jenny got them all into the spirit fairly quickly. She insisted the others simply listen and then invited them to ask questions. When one or two of them started to talk about a similar experience, Jenny gently, but firmly, reminded them this was Alex's turn. All they had to do was to ask questions so they understood what she really meant. After that, it was easy.

She invited them to say what they had understood by giving a brief summary. Jenny prepared little notepads and asked them to write down a sentence or two. She was amazed how readily they did this. When Nicolas first suggested this, Jenny thought she could never ask, that if she did, her friends would never do it. But as she talked this through with Nicolas, she recognized these were her old tapes playing. If she simply trusted it, something would happen. It did!

One by one, the women read back to Alex what they heard her say. While the essence was the same from each of them, there were often subtle, and occasionally significant differences. When Alex wrote down and read back her own summary, it was clear she was moved by this experience and gained a new insight into what seemed quite a dilemma for her.

Next, Jenny asked them all, except Alex, to write down what they would do as though they were Alex – putting themselves into her shoes. Once again, they energetically carried out this task and read back what they wrote. Alex asked to hear them all a second time, then, on Jenny's bidding, wrote down her own action and read this back.

"That was amazing," Alex sighed after she said what she would do. "I discovered more about myself from having been heard by everyone than if I'd read a hundred self-help books. Thanks everyone, and especially you Jenny."

"There's one more thing," said Jenny. "Now I want everyone to write down what you got from the story Alex told us. What are the implications for you?"

"What do you mean?" asked Marge. "Do you want us to say how we were impacted by what Alex said? Or connect it to one of our own experiences?"

"Well, both I think," replied Jenny. "Don't forget, this is the first time I've tried this, so we're all experimenting."

There was silence while all of them wrote in their notepads.

Lying in bed, going through her own words in her head, Jenny reflected on what she had written. Alex talked about the difficult time she was going through with her sick cat. At first, she thought people would laugh at her, so she didn't talk about it much. But she had this cat for nearly twenty years. He seemed to be nearing the end of his life. Alex spoke about this, relating it to the time her grandmother died. How hard it was to show her emotions because the rest of her family wanted her to "be strong."

Jenny suddenly gained a personal insight. Like Alex, Jenny discovered it hard to express her emotions of loss. There was the loss of or rejection by Peter. But mostly, her sense of bereavement was of the loss of her own self-confidence and belief. She wrote that down and read it to the others. Each of the women at the table shared a piece of herself that Jenny had never heard.

Slipping into sleep, Jenny felt a sense of belonging that she had seldom, if ever, known.

Recipe for a Group Dialogue

1. Presentation. Invite one person to talk about something of personal interest.

2. Clarification. Invite the others present to ask questions just to clarify what the speaker means about specific aspects. Don't allow people to go into their own "stories" or explanations.

3. Summaries. Ask all present, except the speaker, to give a succinct summary of what they have understood. This is best if they write it down first and read it back.

4. Speaker's summary. When everyone else has given a summary, the speaker gives her own summary.

5. Action. Ask each person to say what she or he would do. This is not the same as advice-giving. Each person is invited to imagine being the speaker.

6. Speaker's action. Now the speaker says what s/he will do, or has understood differently, as a result of having heard from everyone else.

7. Implications. Everyone is now asked to consider the implication for him/herself in relation to the issue that the speaker has presented.

A dinner party made easy (for seven)
Fresh Cheddar Scones

Mmmm, dinner parties. Is it a heroic undertaking or an easy flash of the pan? This recipe was designed and tested on four of my girlfriends and three of my boyfriends. Preparing the pie pastry and making the filling a day in advance was a great way to even out my workload on the evening of the party. My stew was prepared the morning of my dinner party and reheated on low an hour before guests arrived with a total of two hours on the stove. Finally, as the stew went back on the stove, I made the scone dough but did not add the liquid! The secret to great scones and awesome entertaining, make your dinner look effortless. This provides much entertainment for both you and your guests! Combine your scone recipe ½ hour before eating, pop in the oven. Remove, serve up dinner, et voila! RH

2 cups unbleached flour
¼ cup granulated sugar
1 tb. baking powder
½ tsp. salt
½ cup cold unsalted butter, diced
1 large egg
¼ cup milk
5 tb. 36 percent cream
1/3 cup grated cheddar cheese

Method:

1. In a food processor, place flour, sugar, baking powder, and salt. Pulse to mix. Add butter and pulse until flour resembles a coarse meal 8-10 times.

2. Add egg, milk, and cream. Pulse until mixture is just combined. Do not over mix or scones will be tough.

3. Scoop about ¼ cup onto a greased or parchment paper lined pan about 2 inches apart. Sprinkle grated cheddar cheese on top.

4. Bake for 15 minutes at 425⁰F.

Black Bean and Sausage Stew

4 tb. olive oil
1½ lb. lamb sausage, cut diagonally into 1/2 inch slices
1 onion diced
2 carrots, sliced
2 celery stalks, sliced
7 garlic cloves, minced
32 oz. can black beans
1½ liters chicken stock
2 bay leaves
3 tsp. thyme, dried 1 tb. fresh
1 tsp. rosemary, dried 1 tb. fresh
Salt and pepper to taste

Method:

1. Heat 2 tb. oil in large saucepan over medium high heat until hot but not smoking. Brown sausage, about 6-10 minutes. Remove sausage and place in a bowl.

2. Add onion, carrots, and celery to pot.

3. Stir in garlic, black beans, stock, bay leaf, and herbs if using dried ones. Season with salt and pepper and bring to a boil.

4. Reduce heat and simmer on med. low heat for 30-40 minutes.

5. Return sausage to the pot, add herbs. Sausage should be hot.

Individual Apple Ginger Pies

2 large eggs
2/3 cup plus 2 tb. granulated sugar
2 tsp. fresh lemon juice
¼ cup plus 3 tb. unbleached white flour
1½ tsp. ground ginger
¼ tsp salt
9 tb. unsalted butter
1 vanilla bean, scraped or 1 tsp. vanilla extract
3 tb. fresh ginger, peeled, and finely grated
3 Granny Smith apples, peeled and cut into 1/4 inch dice
Pie pastry to follow

Method:

1. Whisk together eggs and 2/3 cup plus 1 tb. granulated sugar in a medium bowl until thick and pale yellow.

2. Whisk in lemon juice, then flour, ground ginger, and a pinch of salt. Put aside.

3. Put 8 tb. butter, vanilla bean seeds or vanilla extract, and grated ginger in a small saucepan. Cook over medium high heat until butter foams and browns, about 5 minutes. Pour mixture through a fine sieve into a bowl and discard solids. Whisk constantly, pour butter mixture into egg mixture, and whisk until combined.

3. Melt remaining tb. butter in a medium skillet over medium high heat. Add apples and remaining ¼ tsp. salt and 1 tb. sugar cook, stirring until apples are soft; 5 minutes. Let cool, about 10 minutes. Fold pear mixture into egg mixture. Fold pear mixture into egg mixture; set filling aside.

4. Roll out dough on a lightly floured surface to 1/8 inch thick. Using a paring knife or a 5-inch round cookie cutter, cut 8 discs and gently press into a standard sized muffin tin, making pleats around edges and gently pressing to seal. Fill each with 6 tb. filling. Refrigerate 45 minutes.

5. Pre-heat oven to 375⁰F. Bake pies until crusts and filling are golden brown; 25-30 minutes. Let cool in tins on a wire rack about 30 minutes. Unmold and let cool completely on rack. Just before serving, dust with icing sugar.

Pie Pastry

2½ cups unbleached white flour
1 tsp. sugar
1 tsp. salt
12 tb. cold unsalted butter, cut into small pieces
¼ cup cold vegetable shortening
1 tb. white vinegar
¼-1/3 cup ice water

Method:

1.   Pulse flour, sugar, and salt in the bowl of a food processor. Pulse until mixture resembles coarse meal.

2.   With processor running, pour in vinegar, then ¼ cup ice water, process until dough comes together. (If dough is still crumbled add up to ¼ cup more ice water 1 tb. at a time.)

3.   Pat dough into a disk and wrap in plastic. Refrigerate dough until cold, at least 1 hour and up to 1 day.

8. CREATE YOUR REAL STORY
What's on your plate?

Your journey is your story.
Tell it and share the miracle of the
universe seen through your eyes.

"You have ten minutes," intoned Nicolas. "I'll leave you to it."

Jenny stared at the blank sheet of paper in front of her and at the oddly shaped rock that Nicolas placed beside it. The task Nicolas gave her was to write a story as though she were the rock. She thought she could draw it. Writing a story about it was another matter. But she trusted Nicolas. What was more important, she trusted herself now. This was recipe number six, Storytelling. She lost count. All she knew was each recipe made an impact on her, although she had no idea how writing about a rock would make a difference.

She picked up the rock, turned it over, and ran her fingers over its partly smooth and partly rough surface. She examined the varied shades and unusual markings. She put it down, picked up her pen and began to write.

'I'm solid,' she began, 'yet from the outside, you would think I have no clear substance. On the outside, I am colored with shades I accumulated from centuries of development. I am smooth and round on one side, while on the other side, my rough edges can rub away at your skin until it wears you away. Both these sides and all my shades make me what I am and give me the quality that make me the unique rock I am.

'I originated from deep within the earth and was catapulted into a strange universe when a volcanic eruption hurtled me into space. I was separated from the much larger rock I had been a part of. I lay on the ground for many years, until a boy picked me up and threw me, this time with much less force, into a river. Over many more years, the flowing water smoothed away one side of me, but the other side resisted and remained rough. After many more years, the river was diverted and I found myself once again on dry land in the company of thousands of other small rocks. I talked to many of them, but I never found one who had a story like mine. I felt lonely.

'One day, a man and a woman walked by. The woman picked me up and gave me to the man. "Here," she said. "Take this rock and keep it forever. It has a story to tell, and you will offer it to others so they can unlock that story."

'Now I have a place of honor on a table, where people come by, pick me up, and discover my story.'

Jenny sat back, looking up just as Nicolas walked back into the room. "Looks like you've finished," he observed. "Would you like to read it out to me?"

She felt a little coy, but held up the paper and read it aloud. She felt strange reading it and heard the faint tremor in her voice, an odd vibration that seemed to flow through her body.

"That's great for someone who just told me she couldn't write, Jenny," Nicolas told her. "Do you see any connections between the rock you just wrote about and your own story?"

Jenny looked through what she had written. "Well, I guess you could say I feel fairly solid on the inside, but you can't always tell that on the outside. I suppose I have accumulated a lot of characteristics, like the shades. Come to think of it, color and painting are pretty important to me. Oh, and of course, the smooth and the rough parts. I know I have those sides to me. If you rub me up the wrong way, I can be pretty harsh, but mostly, I suppose I'm harsh with myself."

She looked more closely. "Oh, and I think I'm much more able to say now that all those parts of me, including the parts I don't like, are what make me unique. I'm starting to accept the bits I don't like, because without them, I wouldn't be me."

"Tell me about the volcanic eruption and the boy who threw you into the river," urged Nicolas gently.

"I've no idea," Jenny responded, and as she did, a wave of sudden realization surged through her. "It's Peter," she blurted out. "The eruption was being taken into a different space when I fell in love and was virtually separated from my family and other friends. Then he threw me over. That's amazing. I had no idea I was writing about that."

Nicolas encouraged her to look at some of the other connections. As she did, she saw in her story how she felt lonely in the company of others. She saw how it was difficult for her to believe that anyone else had the same experience or feelings as hers.

Jenny looked Nicolas in the eyes. "Now I feel it's an honor to share my story with you and my friends. It's like I'm discovering who I am through sharing myself."

"It's an honor for me to hear you," replied Nicolas. "I'd like you to write another story. This time, write about a real story of you as a child. Write it as though it's going on now and you are relating it as it's happening to a friend. I'll leave you for another ten minutes and come back after that time. The rock story was just a warm-up." He lifted his lanky frame from the chair.

Her mind went blank. "I can't remember much of my childhood," she said to his back.

Nicolas turned. "You'll find something." He closed the door gently after him.

'I'm in the kitchen,' she wrote, after a brief scurry around her memory bank. *'Mom gives me a new coloring book with pictures of animals, and for the first time, real watercolor paints instead of crayons. Beginning with the sky, I paint it blue. Then I paint a yellow sun, and it turns green. At first, I'm confused and angry that it turns the wrong color. When I start to paint the animals, I mix different colors and discover that blue and yellow always turn green, red and yellow make orange. I get really excited. It's like magic. I run to show Mommy, but she's busy and doesn't take much notice.*

'After that, it becomes my secret. I make all kinds of shades by mixing different paints. Nobody else knows how to do it. Part of me is thrilled about making this discovery. Another part is hurt and disappointed that Mommy doesn't care. I know if she doesn't, Daddy won't be interested either, because they always say the same.

'I decide to take the paintings and materials up to my room. The hardest thing to move is the jar of water. When I get into my bedroom, I drop the paint box. When I bend to pick it up, the water spills all over the carpet. I don't know what to do; it makes such a mess. I try to mop it up with something, but it gets even worse. I start crying.

'Mommy comes in and is angry with me. "Why did you have to bring it upstairs?" she asks. "What's wrong with the kitchen?" I don't know how to answer her. The reason is I had to do it on my own, so nobody can see my secret. I can't tell her that, so I cry some more. She holds me then, and I feel better.

'Later on, when Daddy is home, they both ask to see my paintings. I show them, but I don't tell them my secret, and they don't realize it.'

. . . .

85

"Wow, what a great story, Jenny. When you're famous, it has to go in the book I'm going to write about you." Marion was the real extrovert of the art class and always a boost to anyone's ego.

This was not the night of art class but rather a night where a few of the group decided to get together to talk about painting and anything else they felt like. Once Jenny told them about her storytelling session, they wanted to know if she had the stories with her. Of course, she did. She read them both and talked about the meanings and connections she made.

"Why don't we all write a story?" Marion's suggestion was almost a command, but one that received an enthusiastic response.

An hour went by. It seemed like a minute to all of them. Stephanie was the last of the five to read her story and talk about what it meant to her. They laughed, cried, and gained inspiration from each other, creating a bond that would, Jenny felt certain, last forever. The stories were unique and yet, it seemed, universal. They traveled far and wide and experienced a deeper sense of connection.

As she stepped outside into the cool night air, saying her last goodbyes, Jenny felt the lightness in her. She was discovering her inner peace. Now, she was bringing others with her. If only she could take Serge on the same journey. Ah well; he had to want to go there.

. . . .

The journey Serge was on was on a ski slope. He decided to join the group of regular weekend ski enthusiasts from work. Serge was not a bad skier, but he normally preferred to ski alone or with one or very few people.

He persuaded himself to go because he had the feeling this was going to be the last time he would be invited. He declined each time Grant or one of the others asked him to go. He had the distinct impression he was making himself more and more of an outsider. When Grant came past his desk and waved the list at him, there was clearly no expectation Serge would agree. He wasn't quite sure why, but he surprised himself and Grant when he said yes.

It was hard work. The skiing was fine, with a crisp, fresh snow that enabled him to ski at his best. The hard work came afterwards, when they all got together in the bar and restaurant to tell their skiing stories, which moved onto stories of other sporting activities, vacations, driving adventures, jokes, and office rumors.

He clutched a glass of beer. He was more alone here than if he'd stayed at home. Once more, the old feeling of confusion settled on him. He found the conversation and connections here superficial and unsatisfying. Yet, he was uncomfortable with, even afraid of, Jenny's desire to talk at deeper levels.

Serge looked into the bottom of his glass before draining the last drops. He sighed, searching the cheerful faces. There was only one conclusion. He was always going to feel out of place. He was a loner and a loser.

Sunday evening, when he arrived back at his apartment, Serge called Jenny.

"Hi. It's me," he told her lamely.

Jenny's sounded excited and happy. "How was the weekend? Did you have a wonderful time? I hope you haven't injured anything."

He wasn't sure how he was going to do this. Serge swallowed and plunged on, ignoring her enquiries and the lilt in her voice.

"Jenny, I have to tell you something."

Silence.

"I have to say I've realized something this weekend. I am too much of a loner for any kind of a relationship. I just want you to know that now, before we go too far. I'm saying that I just feel that…oh heck. Help me out."

"Oh Serge, I wish I could, but you have to find out yourself what the right thing is for you. I do hear you, though, and it's okay. If you want to break off our relationship, I understand, and I'll respect it. I wish you wouldn't because I really think we have a great chance here. But we'd both have to believe that."

When he put down the phone, Serge slumped into his armchair, his head in his hands.

A few miles away, Jenny looked into the mirror, watching as the tears ran down her face and into the corners of her smile.

Recipe for Storytelling

1. Select an object at random.

2. Write its story, as though you were the object.

3. Read the story out loud, preferably to someone else.

4. Ask yourself what the story you have written tells you about yourself.

5. Next, write a story from your childhood memories.

6. Read the story out loud.

7. Ask yourself how the story connects to who you are now.

What's on your plate?
A storybook meal
Afghan Home-Style Nan Bread

During my years in the food industry, I have had the fortunate opportunity of working with people from different parts of the world. Often these co-workers would serve up a "homestyle" meal for a staff dinner. Papaya salads are delicious and nutritious. Well worth trying.   RH

This meal is designed for 4-6 servings.

2 tsp. dried yeast
½ cup warm water (105-115⁰F)
1 cup well chilled plain full fat yogurt
1 cup boiling water
Approximately 5½ cups whole wheat bread flour
2 tb. corn or safflower oil
2 tsp. sea salt
6 tb. white sesame seeds

Method:

1.   Sprinkle yeast over the warm water in a large bowl, stirring to dissolve.

2.   Place the yogurt in a medium bowl and gradually stir in the boiling water. Let cool to a tepid temperature. (105-115⁰F)

3.   Stir the yogurt mixture into the yeast mixture. Stir in 3 cups flour, ½ cup at a time. Stir for 2 minutes in the same direction. Cover sponge with plastic wrap and let stand for 30 minutes.

4.   Sprinkle oil and salt onto the sponge. Mix in enough of the remaining flour, ½ cup at a time, to form a dough. Turn out onto a lightly floured surface and knead until smooth and elastic, adding more flour if the dough is sticky, about 10 minutes.

Continue...

5.   Wash out and lightly oil the large bowl. Add the dough, turning to coat the entire surface. Cover with a damp kitchen towel or plastic wrap and let rise until doubled in volume, about 1 hour.

6.   Position the oven racks in the lower third of the oven and place a baker's stone or a 10 x 14-inch baking sheet in the oven to preheat. Preheat oven to 450°F.

7.   Punch dough down. Divide into 6 pieces. Using lightly floured hands, flatten each piece on a lightly floured work surface into a 4-5 inch round. Cover the rounds with a kitchen towel or plastic wrap and let rest for 10 minutes.

8.   Lightly flour the backside of a large baking sheet. Working with one dough round at a time, roll out on a lightly floured surface until the dough begins to stretch (keep the remaining dough covered). Brush the flour from the work surface and sprinkle 1 tb. of the sesame seeds onto the work surface. Lay the dough on the seeds and roll out into a 6 x 10-inch rectangle. Turn the dough over. Using the tip of a sharp knife, cut 5 one-inch slits evenly spaced around the dough, radiating out from the center like sun rays or flower petals.

9.   Slide the dough onto the prepared baking sheet and transfer to the preheated sheet or stone in the oven.

10.   Bake until the top begins to brown, about 5 minutes. Transfer the bread to a rack. Repeat with the remaining dough rounds and sesame seeds.

Serve warm or at room temperature.

Papaya and Peanut Salad

2 cups packed grated green or semi-ripe papaya
½ cup unsalted peanuts, dry-roasted and roughly chopped
2 limes, juiced
3 tb. shredded unsweetened coconut
2 tb. fresh cilantro, minced
1 jalapeno, finely chopped
½ tsp. sea salt
Butter leaf lettuce for serving

Method:

1.   Bring 2 cups of water to a boil in a medium saucepan. Toss in the grated papaya, return to boil, and turn off heat. Let papaya sit in the water for 2 minutes and strain.

2.   In a large bowl combine peanuts, papaya, limejuice, and coconut. Mix in the cilantro, jalapeno and salt. Chill in the refrigerator for 30 minutes.

3.   To serve, mound the salad on a plate lined with lettuce leaves.

Chicken and Apricot Curry

2 tb. peanut or olive oil
½ cup shallots
2 tb. Thai red curry paste
2 tb. ginger, minced
1 tsp. sea salt
½ tsp. pepper
4 chicken breasts
2 14-oz. cans coconut milk
½ cup dried apricots, cut in half
¼ cup mango chutney
¾ cup fresh cilantro, chopped fine

Method:

1. Heat oil in a medium-large skillet with lid. Sweat onions until translucent.

2. Add curry paste, ginger, salt and pepper, stir until spices are fragrant.

3. Add chicken breasts and brown.

4. Add coconut milk, apricots, and chutney. Cover and simmer for 25 minutes. Chicken should be tender.

5. Stir in fresh cilantro and serve over hot, steaming basmati or jasmine rice.

Crisp Anise Cookies

1½ cups unbleached flour
¾ tsp. baking powder
¼ tsp. sea salt
½ cup unsalted butter
1/3 cup plus 2 tb. sugar
1 large egg yolk
2 tb. brandy
½ tsp. aniseed, toasted

Method:

1. Preheat oven to 325⁰F. Sift flour, baking powder, and sea salt into a small bowl.

2. Beat butter and 1/3 cup sugar in large bowl until light. Beat in egg yolk, brandy, and aniseed. Add dry ingredients and beat just until a smooth dough forms.

3. Spread remaining 2 tb. sugar on a small plate. Roll dough out on a lightly floured surface to about a ¼-inch thickness.

4. Using a round 2-inch cookie cutter, cut out cookies.

5. Place cookies on the sugared plate, transfer cookies; sugared side up onto an un-greased baking sheet. Bake cookies until bottom and edges are golden, about 20 minutes. Transfer cookies to a rack and cool.

9. You and your dreams
The symbols in your food

You dream what you may not dare to think. Allow your dreams to teach you the meaning of the deepest reaches of your inner space.

She lifted the gate as she pressed down the latch, knowing its slight stiffness. It swung back and she turned to close it carefully before walking up the path, counting each flagstone as though there would be one more or less this time.

As she raised her foot at the first step, the door opened ahead of her. Her father stood, holding his Sunday newspaper. His other arm was open to offer and receive a hug. Her mother stood just behind him. It was like being at a receiving line at a wedding.

"Hi Dad, hi Mom; can we get in out of the cold?" She immediately scolded herself, hearing the inside voice that questioned why she spoke so sharply. The warmth of their house, her home, seemed to help her to relax. She now had the ability to observe what was going on within her and to choose to act differently.

They questioned her, of course, about her work, her health, and her painting. Jenny answered all their questions as fully as she could, before they moved on to the next subject, without once feeling defensive, even when the topic finally arrived, as she knew it would, at Serge. When she told her parents she and Serge were no longer seeing each other, she saw in their eyes the expression of anxiety and concern that she came to expect.

"It's all right, you know," she assured them. "People do go through this, and I'm fine. I really like Serge. I'm sorry we've broken up, but he is going through a difficult time personally. I think he's been hurt in relationships, just like I have. The difference is I have dealt with it, and he is still coming to grips with what he wants in life. I wish he'd get some help, because I'm not the person to give it to him."

Her father gave a kind of non-committal grunt. Her mother said nothing. But Jenny saw in them a different look. It seemed to her a look of admiration.

The meal her mom cooked, as always, was divine. The caramel coffee meringues topped it off.

"These are just a dream," Jenny said, and it reminded her suddenly of the dream she had the night before. Normally, she would have said nothing about it. Today was different.

"Speaking of dreams, I had this really interesting one last night. I was in this large room with a great domed ceiling. It was like a castle, or an art gallery, because the walls were covered with portraits of people and so was the ceiling. As I gazed upward, the ceiling seemed to open up, and there were millions of stars. I floated up through the opening until I was high above looking down at me. It was weird. I was up in the sky, looking down, surrounded by stars, and I was in the room looking up. Then the stars started turning into bubbles. When they burst, more stars popped out of them. I have no idea what it meant. I'll find out when I talk to Nicolas this week. He said we're going to look at a dream and asked me to remember one. Funny thing is I don't seem to remember my dreams much, and as soon as he asked me, I remember one."

She was aware her parents shied away from discussing her sessions with Nicolas. They saw it as a sign of weakness, that there was something wrong with their daughter and should not be discussed. Now here, she openly admitted she was going to tell him about her dream.

"I always thought dreams were interesting," replied her mother. "Ever since I was a little girl and heard the story of Joseph and the dreams he had. Do you remember that John?"

Jenny's father stirred. "Yes. Yes, he had a story about stars. Then there were the seven sheaves of corn and the cattle. He upset his brothers, but he told the pharaoh and saved the country from drought, I recall."

Jenny felt her jaw drop open and clamped it shut.

It was dark when she left the house. "Great lunch, Mom. Good stories, Dad. Lovely to see you both. Thanks for a wonderful conversation."

The next day she related to Nicolas the dream she described to her parents.

"I call this Dreamtime," he said. "It's your next recipe. Like all the others, you can try this at home. Here's a large sheet of paper and colored pens and pencils. I know the art material is not as sophisticated as you're used to. I'd like you to draw your dream, or a segment of it, as closely as you recollect it."

She was in her element, drawing the room, the portraits, the stars turning into bubbles, and the two figures that were her in the room and in the sky.

"That's perfect," said Nicolas when she finished. "Now imagine each of the symbols in your dream has something to say. For example, what is the room saying about itself? What do the portraits and the stars say? Include yourself and everything in your picture. Write it down as though this is one of those cartoon strips with the words coming out of their heads or wherever their heads might be if they had them."

This was a littler harder. When Jenny completed the task, Nicolas asked her to number each of the scenes she created in the sequence in which they took place in her dream. Finally, he asked her to read the words out loud.

She surveyed her work. "The first is the room itself, which says, 'I'm light and spacious, with plenty of room to hold these paintings and so Jenny can move around.' Next are the portraits. They are saying 'we are the faces of your people and here to remind you who you are.' I hadn't quite understood that in the dream, but I'm sure that's what they would be saying. Then Jenny in the room is saying, 'I'm happy gazing at the pictures and the ceiling and being in this wonderful space.' Next the ceiling says, 'I'm opening up so you can see the stars.' Then I float through the ceiling."

Jenny read the words to herself and turned to Nicolas. "I'm beginning to get this. Jenny in the sky is saying, 'I am flying into space, watching all around me and seeing myself on the ground.' The stars say, 'We surround you, lighting you up,' then the bubbles say, 'We are bursting out with even more stars.' I thought I was beginning to understand it, but I'm not sure now. What do I do now?"

"I'm going to read it out to you again Jenny, only this time I want you to imagine the words are your own. So instead of the room speaking, it is really you. I may have to change it slightly to make sense of it, but the meaning will be the same."

Nicolas took the sheet and read to her. "I'm light and spacious, with plenty of room for my paintings and so I can move around. I hold the faces of my people to remind me who I am. I'm happy gazing and being in this wonderful space. I'm opening up so I can see the stars. I am flying into space, watching all around me and seeing myself on the ground. I surround myself, lighting me up. I am bursting out with even more stars."

97

Neither Jenny nor Nicolas said anything for a full minute. Jenny broke the silence. "That's what I said, isn't it? That's what my dream said to me. It's true. I do feel light, especially with all the weight I've lost. I can move around now. My paintings are important to me. So is my family. They always remind me who I am. I'm happy just being in this space, and I'm certainly opening up. We have been talking about that journey into inner space. I feel like I'm flying and bursting with more energy and light than I ever had. Wow! That's amazing. I can't wait to have another dream!"

. . . .

Serge stirred from a deep slumber. The inside of his mouth felt like a strip of sandpaper. He had to get a drink. He pushed himself up and slid his legs out of bed, then stumbled into the bathroom. He splashed cold water onto his face, slurped some up, and gargled. Finally, he filled a glass and drank it in one gulp.

He checked the time. It was 2:25. He switched off the bathroom light, plunged himself into darkness, and lurched back into the bedroom. As he pulled the covers over his body, he recalled the edges of the dream that must have awoken him. No wonder he felt thirsty! He was in a desert.

The more he concentrated, the more he remembered. He charged to an oasis, which got further and further away. Sometimes he rode a camel, sometimes a tank. However fast he traveled, or whatever mode of transport he used, the oasis seemed to move faster.

"What was that all about?" he wondered out loud. The images stayed with him for a long time until he fell back into a restless sleep.

Recipe for Dreamtime

1. Draw your dream.

2. Write the words each object or symbol in your dream is saying (or would say).

3. Number each scene in sequence.

4. Read the words out loud, preferably to someone else.

5. Read it again, or preferably have someone else read it, this time as though you are each of the symbols.

6. This is what your dream is saying, or rather, what you are unconsciously saying to yourself.

7. Think, or talk about, what you appreciate about your dream and what, if anything, you want to change.

A dREAM mEAl
Fennel and Endive Salad with Orange Vinaigrette

Ahhh, dreams, serene, magical. This menu has been designed to lift your spirit and comfort the soul. Thin slices of delicate sweet fennel open the taste buds. Earthy mushrooms provide grounding for inspiration and the coffee meringue – may it provide a porthole for your imagination and creativity. RH

This meal has been designed for 4 servings.

2 navel oranges
1½ tsp. white-wine vinegar
¼ tsp. sea salt
¼ tsp. black pepper
3 tb. olive oil
1 fennel bulb
2 Belgian endives, trimmed (go ahead, give them a try!)

Method:

1.   Finely grate enough zest from both oranges to measure 1 tb. Squeeze juice of one orange into a large bowl. Whisk in zest, vinegar, sea salt, pepper, and oil until well combined.

2.   Remove the peeling from the second orange and cut into 4 rounds.

3.   Cut fennel bulbs lengthwise into very thin slices with a slicer or sharp knife. Cut the base of the endive and arrange 3 leaves on 4 plates.

4.   Place 1 orange slice over the endive spears. Then toss your nicely, thin sliced fennel with the orange dressing and place a at the base of the orange slice for a nice presentation. Drizzle any remaining dressing evenly over each salad.

Wild Mushroom Lasagna

Béchamel sauce
3 tb. butter
2½ tb. unbleached flour
3 cups whole milk, heated
1 garlic clove, smashed
¾ tsp. sea salt
½ tsp. black pepper

Mushroom tomato sauce
2 cups boiling stock (beef, chicken, or vegetable)
2 5-oz. pkgs. dried procini mushrooms
2 large portobello mushrooms, sliced thin
1 cup sliced button mushrooms
1 cup onion, diced
2 tb. olive oil
2 14-oz. cans diced tomatoes
1 tsp. sugar
¼ cup basil, chopped fresh
½ tsp. sea salt

Assembling lasagna
12 long dried lasagna noodles
1¾ cups finely grated parmigiano-reggiano cheese

To make béchamel sauce:

1.   Heat butter in a 2-quart heavy saucepan over medium-low heat until melted.

2.   Add flour and cook 'roux' stirring continuously.

3.   Add hot milk, whisking vigorously.

4.   Add garlic, sea salt, and pepper.

5.   Bring to boil, stirring, reduce heat and simmer for 20 minutes. Stir occasionally. Remove garlic.

Continue...

To make mushroom tomato sauce:

1. Pour boiling stock over porcini mushrooms and let stand 20 minutes to soften. Remove and squeeze access liquid. Pour soaking water through coffee filter to remove grit and save the liquid. Chop porcini mushrooms.

2. Sweat onion in olive oil in a medium pot over medium heat. Add mushrooms and cook for 15 minutes

3. Stir in tomatoes with juice, sugar, and liquid, and 1 tb. basil. Cover and simmer, stirring frequently, for 30 minutes. Stir in sea salt and remaining basil.

Assemble and bake lasagna:

1. Cook noodles in a large pot with boiling water, 1 tsp. sea salt and 1 tb. olive oil until al dente about 8-10 minutes. Drain and pat dry with paper towel or kitchen towel.

2. Put oven rack in middle position and preheat to 425°F.

3. Spread 1/3 of the béchamel sauce on the bottom of a buttered 13 x 9-inch baking dish.

4. Cover the béchamel sauce with lasagna noodles.

5. Spread 1/3 tomato mushroom sauce evenly over noodles. Sprinkle with 1/3 cup cheese.

6. Assemble 3 layers in total finishing with béchamel sauce and then parmesan cheese.

7. Bake, uncovered, until lasagna is bubbling and top is browned. 30-35 minutes. Let stand at room temperature at least 15 minutes before cutting.

Caramel Coffee Meringues

3/4 cup sugar
2 tb. instant-espresso powder
3 large egg whites at room temperature
1/2 cup water
1/2 cup heavy cream

To make meringues:

1. Put oven rack in lower third of oven and preheat to 500⁰F. Lightly oil 4-5 oz. ramekins (small individual oven proof ceramic dishes).

3. Stir together 1/2 cup sugar and 1 tb. espresso powder in a small bowl.

4. Beat whites with pinch of sea salt in large bowl with electric mixer until soft peaks are formed.

3. Add sugar mixture a bit at a time to the egg whites, beating, and increasing speed to high and continuing to beat until whites hold a stiff glossy peak.

4. Spoon meringue into ramekins, forming gentle swirling peaks in tops. Arrange ramekins on a baking sheet and bake until meringues are slightly puffed and a shade darker, 4-5 minutes

5. Transfer ramekins to a rack and cool for 30 minutes then chill for at least 3 hours. (Meringues will deflate slightly and pull away from sides of ramekins.)

Continue...

To make syrup:

1. Stir together ¼ cup water and 1 tb. espresso powder in a small metal bowl.

2. Bring remaining ¼ cup sugar and remaining ¼ cup water to a boil in a small pot with a heavy bottom. Stir until sugar is dissolved, washing down any crystals from side of pan with a pastry brush dipped in water. Boil syrup without stirring,until mixture is a deep golden caramel.

3. Remove from heat and carefully pour in espresso mixture (liquid will bubble and steam), stir until well combined, cool for at least 20 minutes.

To make topping and serve meringues:

1. Beat cream with electric mixer until soft peaks form.
2. Drizzle each meringue with 1 tb. syrup and whip cream.

10. Mirror, mirror on the wall
Your food reflects you

The further you travel into your soul, the greater and more exciting the journey will be.

"Now I really want you to look into inner space," said Nicolas. "You're ready for this. It's the eighth recipe for your journey, and it's simply called The Mirror, because that's what it is."

He reached up and took a wooden-framed mirror from the wall. Jenny had admired it before for its simplicity. She often glanced at her reflection in it as she walked into his office. She noticed now she was happier to see herself than when she first came.

It was heavier than she thought. She held the mirror in her hands, resting it on her lap, tilting it so her face stared back at her, looking a little self-conscious. Ten minutes was a long time. That's what Nicolas had asked of her. She was to look into the mirror for ten minutes, saying whatever came to her.

Her first reaction was to put her hand to her hair, flicking it back into place. She suddenly felt shy and a little foolish. The feeling was mirrored back to her. She composed herself, breathed deeply, and looked into her eyes.

"You," she said softly, "are beautiful. I've never seen you so strong. You have been on an amazing journey to get here, and now, I've discovered you. You have such determination. I'm proud of you. Oh, and those tears in your eyes are something to be proud of too. You have learned a lot. You learned you have an inner strength. You don't have to depend on anyone else to say you're okay. You're fine just the way you are. When I take a different view," and here Jenny held the mirror away from her, "I see that you look great all over. You've lost weight without even trying too hard. It happened when you started to believe in yourself and no longer had to feed yourself to compensate for what you thought you didn't have."

Jenny leaned forward, peered even more intently into her eyes. She never looked at herself this way; never saw beyond her physical self. She was looking into her soul. This is what Nicolas meant when he talked about inner space. This was the great exploration. She was so close to the mirror now that it misted faintly from her breath. "Thank you for being you," she whispered. "I love you."

The gust of February wind caught her as she walked to her car. She had only one more session left with Nicolas. As she drove home, she thought about the things she talked about and how she had transformed almost everything in her life although, little had changed on the outside. She still lived in the same place, had the same job; she even, it seemed, had no boyfriend. On the other hand, she was painting and had a new circle of friends. She'd lost weight and felt a whole lot better.

Turning onto her street, she knew the important changes were much more subtle and significant. Looking into the mirror had shown her that.

Jenny turned the key in the door, picked up the mail, and dropped it on the hall table, as she struggled out of her coat. She made herself a light meal, turned on the CD player with a few of her favorite discs, and picked up the book she was reading. This would be a quiet relaxing evening.

A couple of hours later, as she headed for bed, she noticed the mail and carried it with her to the bedroom. A couple of bills, an offer to subscribe to a magazine, and what looked like a card. Puzzled, she opened it. It was a Valentine's card from Serge.

. . . .

The waiter flicked his cloth lightly and expertly over the chair, for no apparent reason, and pulled the seat back for Jenny. He gestured to Serge that he should sit in the opposite one, then deftly lit the small candle in the center of the table.

Serge said little, apart from telling Jenny how lovely she looked, and how happy he was to see her.

After the waiter poured a glass of wine for each of them from the bottle they ordered, Serge cleared his throat.

"I've been thinking a lot," he began. He seemed to run out of words. She waited.

"I've seen you blossom so much over the past few months. I know you were trying to get me to become more, well, open, I suppose. I was wondering if," he paused long enough for Jenny to wonder if he had forgotten what he was going to say, or more likely that he didn't know how to say it.

"Do you want to ask me something?" she asked. She felt nervous and a little faint, picked up her glass and took a sip. She replaced it and put her hands on her lap.

"Yes. I want to ask if you think it would be a good idea for me to go and see Nicolas."

Jenny sat very still. The blessed waiter saved her, serving them their starter tomato and peach salad with a flourish and a "bon appétit." She was ready by then, her mind having had a brief conversation with her heart.

"Serge, if you are willing to do that, I think it's a wonderful idea. It's not easy, but I think it will make all the difference. I know it has for me."

"I've been thinking about it a lot since we kind of split up," he confided. "I know how much it meant to you. I really admire you for what you've done. I know you were trying to get me to do this stuff too. I always shied away from it. It felt a little too close to the mark sometimes. I don't know, I suppose I wasn't ready to admit things to myself. Then the other night I had this dream. I suddenly realized I'm trying to get to an ideal place in my life. I want inner peace, I guess. It gets further away the more I try to find it. When I think of you, I see someone who has found it from the inside. So I thought, well why not give it a try?"

Jenny sat silent. This was for Serge to figure out. She kept thinking of the Valentine's card he sent her and his phone call to ask her out this evening. She was aware of her disappointment at how this was going, but she was also proud that Serge was taking this direction. She relaxed, feeling lighter, as though suddenly relieved of a burden.

"You are so right," she said. "I'm so happy you are doing this and that you're doing it for you and not for me. Whatever happens between us, know you will find what you are looking for when you talk about it with Nicolas."

Serge put down his fork and held his hand across the table. Jenny put her hand in his. He held her gaze, looking intently into her eyes. The world stopped.

"I think you are the most wonderful person I ever met," he told her. "You are beautiful inside and out. I see someone who has taken charge of herself, who is loving and not needy, independent and creative. Jenny…,"

Serge paused as though he was uncertain what to say or how to say it. "I love you." He had never said this to anyone.

Recipe for the Mirror

1. Find a good mirror that is easy for you to hold.

2. Preferably with another person, whom you trust, or in a small group where all of you are doing this, look into the mirror for a full ten minutes.

3. As you look into your eyes, talk to your reflection about what you see and who you are.

4. When ten minutes are up, and if you are with others, have them ask you questions, while you still look into the mirror. If you are alone, reflect on your experience.

5. Write down what you said and what you felt.

A meal of love
Heirloom Tomatoes and White Peach Salad

Sometimes love is enjoyed for its quality moments and simplicity. One often loves a moment in nature, a wave breaking against a rock, or the soft breathing of a loved one sleeping peacefully. The following recipes follow the same theme. Delicious because of quality, simple preparation, and an abundance of eating enjoyment!   RH

This menu has been designed for 2 servings.

2 large, ripe, juicy Heirloom tomatoes
1 large juicy, ripe white peach
1 small bunch crispy, fresh frisee lettuce
2 plump, red radishes
2 tsp. delicious white balsamic vinegar
Pinch of sweet honey
½ tsp. exotic fleur de sol or other fine sea salt
1 stem freshly picked lemon thyme
1 stem freshly picked lavender
3 tb. organic quality walnut oil or olive oil

Method:

1. Cut tomatoes into wedges.

2. Slice the peaches.

3. Rinse and dry the frisee, pull apart for salad.

4. Slice radish fine.

5. Whisk vinegar, honey sea salt, thyme, and lavender leaves together.

6. Whisk in oil and toss over salad.

7. Enjoy with a loved one, be it yourself or someone else!

Grilled Goat Cheese Sandwiches with Fig Preserves

4 thin slices baguette of great quality, cut diagonally (6 inches)
1-2 tb. butter
¼ cup mild spreadable goat cheese, room temperature
2 tb. fig preserves

Method:

1. Spread 1 side of each baguette slice with butter. Turn over and spread 2 pieces of bread with cheese.

2. Spread the fig preserves on the other two slices.

3. Heat a dry skillet on medium heat. Cook sandwiches on each side about 5 minutes each. They should be golden brown and the cheese wonderfully melted.

   * Fig preserves can usually be found at specialty markets or health food stores.

Chewy Chocolate Brownies

1 cup butter
1/2 cup unsweetened good quality chocolate
2 cups granulated sugar
4 eggs
1 tsp. vanilla extract
1 tsp. unbleached white flour
1/2 tsp. sea salt
1 cup pecans, coarsely chopped

Method:

1. Lightly grease a 13 x 9-inch baking pan. Heat butter over low heat until half melted. Add chocolate and stir until both are completely melted. Remove from heat and stir in sugar.

2. Beat in eggs, one at a time until mixture is shiny. Stir in vanilla, then add flour and salt. Stir in chopped nuts.

3. Pour batter into prepared pan and bake in a preheated 350°F oven for 30 minutes or until the brownies are firm.

4. Cool and enjoy, again with a loved one!

11. Connecting
What your food says about you

You are one with the universe;
one with others.
The more you connect,
the more unique you become.

S he carefully slid the two pieces of paper from the large manila envelope she brought with her. This was to be a 'show and tell' for her final session with Nicolas. He asked her to "bring something of significance," and this is what she found as she rummaged through the memory box she kept in the corner of her cupboard.

When she discovered these two sheets, she knew immediately this was what she wanted to bring with her. They went together, the painting and the poem. She looked at the childish writing and recalled the pride she'd had when she wrote the poem at school and presented it to her parents.

"Well, Jenny, please tell me about your items and what they mean to you. This recipe is the ninth and last in the ones I have to teach you. It's called Connections. There are three kinds of connections you will be making. This first part is your connection to what you have brought as a symbol of something important to you."

Jenny picked up the poem. "I wrote this when I was about seven or eight. When I first saw it yesterday and read it, it felt kind of silly; then I loved what I'd written. I feel as proud of it now as I did when I was little. I even loved that I spelled 'tomorrow' wrong, and that I numbered each verse. I'll read it out to you."

As she read, she felt herself wafting back in time to her childhood and discovered something she had forgotten was in her.

Today

1. *Today I'll sit and think.*

    Tommorow I'll laugh and smile.

    But what shall I do the day after that,

    Who knows? Who knows?

2. *I might be reading a book.*

    I might be sewing a toy

    I might be going out.

    Who knows? Who knows?

3. *But lets just think of today,*

    What a wonderful day it could be,

    Thinking and wondering

    Guessing and pondering,

    Who knows? Who knows?

Jenny Cunningham

Not bad, she thought, except for that one word and the absence of an apostrophe. She knew those were the initial feelings of someone who learned to start with the negatives. She quickly put them aside.

"I haven't read that out loud since the day I wrote it. I can't even remember reading it aloud then, but I probably did. What I see now is how wise I was as a child and how positive and curious. I was a philosopher. People write books about 'living in the now' and it seems very Zen-like. Isn't 'pondering' a great word for an eight-year-old, especially to rhyme with 'wondering'?"

She placed the poem on the table and picked up the painting. She used pencil to draw the outlines and watercolors. It was a picture any small girl might have done, except that in it was a quality that even now, she admired. The subject was of a family, parents, and a little girl standing outside their house. Nothing remarkable there. Two images brought something else to the picture. A tree was so meticulously drawn and painted that each branch and leaf were lifelike miniatures. An angel peering through a fluffy cloud brought tranquility to the picture and offered a sense of safety and comfort to the family beneath.

"I remember being so proud of this picture. I did this when I was nine, after my teacher introduced me to art. Mom stuck it on the fridge and it stayed there for years until we redecorated. I stored it away in my box. What I remember mostly was the feeling I got from painting the tree. Something took over. I started and couldn't stop. I got totally lost in it. It took me hours. I don't think I ever had such an experience since then. That tree, with all its branches and leaves, was so complete. Exquisite is the word I'd use. That was the feeling it brought me when I did it. I wanted life to be like that – exquisite. It brings tears to my eyes."

"And the angel?" enquired Nicolas.

"The angel is my comfort and safety. When I was a child, I thought I always had an angel by my side, looking out for me. I could see her over my bed or walking alongside me whenever I wanted to. I'd forgotten all about her. Lucky I have this picture."

"The poem and the picture – tell me in a few words what they mean to you now," urged Nicolas.

"They remind me of who I really am and what I have in my life," said Jenny, looking up at him quickly.

"You have used the words, 'wise, positive, curious, exquisite, and safe.' Does that describe who you are and what you have?"

She took in the words. Had she really said them? She looked again at the picture and at the poem she wrote so long ago.

"They do feel right. I could never have said that before. I have other things in my life too. I look at the family, my family, in the picture and know I have love. I have always had love from my parents. I've had love in my life before, and I have it now with Serge. I am creative. I see that I use my creativity in many ways, including my job. My boss is always saying how creative I am. In the past, I thought he was being negative, but I know he really meant it. I have a lot of belief in myself now – just like I did when I was eight and nine. I lost it for a long while, but I found it again. I don't know how to thank you, Nicolas. You are my angel now."

She wondered if the slight pinkness on his cheeks betrayed a blush from Nicolas.

"You made some excellent connections between what you have brought today and who you are. The second connection you made is how you are with others. What you shared is your gift to me. My gift to you is to tell you that I see you as someone who has blossomed into that exquisite, wise, creative, and curious self who is now doing what she wanted to do when she came here – listen to herself fully and gain inner peace. That's your third connection, to see how you have completed your contract with yourself. You have heard, understood, and accepted who you are. Now you are ready to embark on the next phase of your life's journey. I know you will continue to create it perfectly, even in the face of challenges that will inevitably be there."

They stood at the door of his office. He held out his hand to her and she hesitated. "I'd like a hug," she told him.

. . . .

"I felt like having an adventurous meal this evening," Serge told her as she walked into his kitchen. "Tell me about your day. This was your last session with Nicolas wasn't it? My first one's tomorrow, so it's almost like taking over."

After they ate, Serge disappeared to find an object that meant something significant. "I'll have done all this before I even see him," he commented as he went upstairs.

"Don't worry," she called, "there's always plenty more to talk about. You'll be amazed."

. . . .

"Hi Sis, it's me."

"You're sounding cheery," came Laurette's voice over the phone. "What's going on? Let me guess. You're back with Jenny. Or you've found another girlfriend."

"You guessed right first time. She's just great. I don't know what made me want to break it off."

The silence on the other end indicated that Laurette didn't know either; unless she was holding back on telling him something he'd rather not hear.

"Anyway," he continued, "I wanted to tell you about what happened last night."

"Are you sure?"

He ignored her tone. "Just listen. I showed Jenny Granddad's army medal for bravery, and I discovered something. I always wondered if I had the kind of courage it took for Granddad and all those other soldiers to do what they did. I think I always believed myself to be a coward. I've taken the safe route mostly and dithered with decisions because I couldn't choose the right thing for me. Well, I do know why I wanted to break things off with Jenny; I was scared. I was scared of making a commitment to someone else when I couldn't even make one to myself. It got me thinking about all the times I've held myself back.

"When I talked to Jenny last night about the medal, I realized being brave doesn't mean not being afraid. I'll bet he was afraid, but he did what he did anyway and risked his own life to save his comrades. Well, my courage might not be like that, but I know that I have it. For the first time, Laurette, I am taking decisions without knowing what's going to happen first, just because it feels right. Wish me luck."

"It's not luck you need," said his wise sister, "but I do wish you everything you wish for yourself."

Recipe for Connections

1. Find something that you own that holds some significance for you.

2. Talk about its connection and meaning to you.

3. Review your contract with yourself and see how you have achieved what you wanted.

4. Give and receive acknowledgements in connection with others around you.

Discovery meal
Red Lentil Hummus

I was watching a friend feed her little girl who was about seven months old at the time. She was in ecstasy at discovering new foods. Every food from that moment on will be a new food introduced. What an adventure we all have with those experiences. The textures, tastes and color, all affect us in that first year or so of life. This meal is written in memory of those first tastes that we all have experienced throughout the years.   RH

Recipes designed for 4-6 servings.

2 cups dried red lentils
1 tb. garlic, minced
½ cup sun dried tomatoes, chopped
3 tb. cumin seeds, dry roasted and ground
2 tb. olive oil
1 tsp. sea salt
½ tsp. pepper

Method:

1.   Rinse lentils in cold water until the water runs clear. Drain.

2.   Cover lentils with clean water and bring to a boil. Add garlic and dried tomatoes. Simmer for 15 minutes. The lentils should be ready to fall apart and the tomatoes should be soft. Drain liquid, cooling it down and saving it for later.

3.   Cool lentil mixture and puree with cumin seeds, salt, and pepper. Slowly add oil in a drizzle with processor or blender running. If hummus is dry, add liquid until smooth.

4.   Adjust seasonings to taste and serve with fresh dilly crackers.

Dilly Crackers

4 cups flour
½ tsp. sea salt
1 tsp. baking soda
1 tsp. sugar
2 tb. butter
1 tsp. dry dill weed
1/3 cup ice water

Method:

1. Combine flour, sea salt, soda, sugar, dill, and butter in food processor, pulse until crumbly.

2. Add ice water slowly until dough forms.

3. On a lightly floured surface, roll dough until flat. Transfer to a parchment paper lined baking sheet and bake at 375⁰F for 10-15 minutes.

Turkey and Sweet Potato Pot Pie with White Cheddar Crust

Filling:
2½ cups water
1 tsp. sea salt
2 cups peeled, diced jewel yam
2 tb. butter
1 medium onion, diced
2 tb. unbleached flour
2½ cups turkey or chicken stock
2 tb. summer savory, fresh minced
1 tsp. black pepper
1 14-oz. can white navy beans
1 tb. fresh parsley or 2 tsp. dried
4 cups cooked diced turkey

Continue...

Method:

1. Boil yam in salted water until just tender, about 8-10 minutes. Remove and place in large bowl.

2. In a medium sauce pan melt butter and sweat onion for 5 minutes. Stir in flour and cook for 1-2 minutes. Slowly add stock, whisking to avoid lumps. Add seasoning and bring to a boil until thick. Simmer 10 minutes.

3. Stir in beans, parsley, turkey, and yams. Place in 8-inch round casserole dish, adjust seasonings to taste.

Pastry:

1 cup unbleached flour
1 tsp. baking powder
½ tsp. sea salt
2 tb. cold butter
1½ cup shredded old cheddar cheese
¼ cup milk

Method:

1. Mix dry ingredients together in a medium metal bowl.

2. Cut butter into dry ingredients with a fork until crumbly.

3. Incorporate cheese, slowly add milk until the dough clings together, adding more if necessary. Do not over mix.

4. Roll dough out and place on top of casserole. Poke with a fork and brush with milk.

12. Recipes for inner peace
Easy and healthy eating

World peace starts with each of us achieving inner peace. Begin the journey now and see how your world changes.

They unwrapped the large, flat parcel, all the time pointlessly advising each other what or what not to do.

Jenny's dad rested it gingerly on his knees, his hands grasping the sides, while her mom peeled off the paper, taking care not to rip it. Jenny knew she'd want to save it for use on some other occasion.

"Happy anniversary," she burst out as the framed painting finally emerged from its cocoon, amidst the expressions of delight from her mom and her father's indeterminate grunts and mutterings.

"Oh Jenny, it's lovely." They both screwed up their eyes, appraising it. Too many seconds went by, before they both spoke at once.

"It's not…?" started her dad. "Is it…did you?" began her mother.

"Of course, it's one of mine," she said, relieved that this was the question behind their eyes. "I painted it especially for you."

The rose was exquisite – yellow, with a pink blush. It was in the process of bursting open; a vibrant, delicate bloom that shone from its dark blue background. She decided on a simple gilt frame, certain where they would want to hang it, and knowing how it would set off the picture to perfection. They had been married for thirty years and still had that large gap on the wall, above the piano.

They looked back and forth at it and at her differently, deferentially now, in awe of her. "You could show this in an exhibition," said her dad. "It'd win first prize."

"It'll go above the piano," her mom determined. "I've been waiting for the right thing for thirty years." They both set about the task of hanging the rose painting in the other room. Jenny decided to leave them to it.

This had been quite a week, and it wasn't over yet. Yesterday she finalized a new agreement with her boss. He called her into his office on Monday. "You handled that Duncan project so well, Jenny. I had faith in you, but you really exceeded my expectations here. I think you're ready for more. How do you feel about heading up a team to take on new prospects? It would mean dealing with all the planning and follow-through, from proposals to design and implementation strategy. What do you think?"

She took a deep breath. "You've asked me two questions," she said. "You asked me how I feel about it and what I think. I feel absolutely excited with the prospect and honored at having been asked. I think the responsibility and workload is huge, and I have lots of questions about my current work and what help and training I can expect."

Reflecting on it now, she was proud of her response and thought Nicolas would have been too. She had the week to think about it. Yesterday she asked for what she wanted and said what she could offer. She asked for a weekly meeting with her boss during the first six months and a monthly one following that so he could coach her through the transition. She asked for three specific training courses she had identified. She asked to pick her own team with his approval. She asked for an assistant for her current work. She asked for a salary increase she believed was appropriate.

He raised his eyebrows at the extent of the salary request and suggested a lower figure. The starting point was more than she thought he would offer. He agreed to her other requests.

"What I'll offer," she said, "is to set up the team, give ourselves three months to plan our strategy, get the training and aim to launch the program. Meanwhile, I'll find and train my assistant and plan to hand over my current workload for the next six months to that person. With your help, I'll set clear targets so we can see how we are doing."

It was a done deal. She was on top of the world. She saw the relief in his eyes.

"As a bonus," he continued as she was leaving his office, "I'll pay for those sessions you had with Nicolas. Well worth the investment. If you want to continue with him to help you over the next year, don't hesitate to ask. After all, he's my coach too. This idea came up when I talked with him."

Jenny stirred from her reverie as her parents called to show her the painting in its place of glory.

As they surveyed it, the doorbell rang. "I have another surprise for you," said Jenny, and went to let in their visitor.

Serge held a bouquet of roses, yellow with a pink blush, in one hand, a bottle of champagne in the other, and a huge smile on his face.

"Mom, Dad," announced Jenny, as she placed her arm around his waist and drew him into the room. "Serge and I are going to get married."

Recipes for Inner Peace
How to Live a Healthy, Easy Life

1. Listening Power. Listen to yourself and others.

2. Learning from Experience. Discover your strengths from what you have experienced.

3. Lifescale. Balance your emotions.

4. The Time Capsule. Converse with your inner child and become who you were always meant to be.

5. Group Dialogue. Listen and learn with others.

6. Storytelling. Create your own wisdom from your real stories.

7. Dreamtime. Find out the personal meaning of your dreams.

8. The Mirror. Look into your soul and celebrate who you are.

9. Connections. Connect with what and who is around you and what is within you.

Healthy easy eating
Green Salad with Balsamic Vinaigrette

Our lives can become so busy at times! I have just opened a restaurant in Halifax, and busy is an understatement. Spending time in my home office means time away from the kitchen at work. A healthy light, easy meal is so important for busy moments. Keep your fridge stocked with fresh veggies and lettuce. Dressings and stir-fries are easy and fun to make. Delicious and healthy barley fudge cookies add a light finish to this meal.   RH

This meal is designed for 2-3 servings.

Mix together your favorite leafy greens and vegetables, fruit and/or nuts. This light dressing works well for a nice, light salad.

1 tsp. honey
1 tsp. Dijon mustard
1 tb. fresh basil, chopped fine (1 tsp. dried)
1 clove garlic, minced
¼ cup balsamic vinegar
2 tb. red wine vinegar
¾ cup light olive oil

Method:
1.   Whisk all ingredients except oil.

2.   Gradually whisk in oil in a slow stream to incorporate.

Tofu and Shrimp Stir-Fry

Tofu is really great frozen and then thawed when cooking dishes such as stir-fries. Once drained of its water it looks a bit like a sponge, so is able to soak up the lovely and flavorful juices that you are about to prepare.

½ lb. firm tofu
6 large shrimp, peeled, cooked, and divined
1 tsp. sesame oil
1 tsp. olive oil
1 tb. garlic, minced
1 tb. ginger, minced
1 carrot, peeled and sliced
1 rib celery, sliced on the bias
1 red pepper, cubed large
1 handfull of snap peas

Sauce:
1 tb. frozen orange juice concentrate
2 tb. soy sauce
1 cup chicken or vegetable stock
2 tb. cornstarch
Sea salt and pepper to taste

Method:
1.   Heat oils in a wok or large sautéing pan.

2.   Add tofu and fry at medium-high heat for about 7-8 minutes, stirring to prevent sticking.

3.   Add garlic and ginger, and turn heat up to high.

4.   Add carrot, celery, and red pepper. Toss vegetables with tofu for 3-4 minutes; the color should be bright, and the vegetables crisp.

5.   Add snap peas, shrimp, and sauce ingredients (mix all sauce ingredients together in a bowl).

6.   The sauce will thicken quickly. Turn down the heat to a medium simmer, cover, 2-3 minutes, adding a bit of stock if the sauce gets too thick.

7.   Remove from heat and serve with your favorite rice.

Barley Fudge Cookies

3/4 cup sunflower oil
1 tsp. vanilla
1 1/3 cup maple syrup
1 cup. soy milk
1/4 cup ground flax seeds
4 cups barley flour
2 tsp. baking soda
1/2 cup dark cocoa or carob
1 cup chocolate chips or carob

Method:

1.   Combine oil, vanilla, maple syrup, milk, and ground flax seeds in a mixer on high speed for 2 minutes. This works the flax seed meal.

2.   Combine dry ingredients in a large bowl. Preheat oven to 350°F.

3.   Add the wet ingredients to dry. Place 1 tb. mounds on a greased cookie sheet.

4.   Bake for 10-12 minutes.

Recipe makes 1 dozen cookies.

The Recipes

Robin Harnish

Robin has been studying healthy diets and cooking for the past 10 years. She has a passion for good food. She founded the company My Good Cook, and through this has been a cooking instructor, personal chef, and presently a small restaurant operator on the Halifax waterfront in Nova Scotia. Robin has won many professional culinary competitions and has traveled as far as Austria to cook.

Other books by WARREN REDMAN

Support for Volunteers (1977) The Volunteer Centre, UK

Working Towards Independence (1979) West-Central, UK

Finding Your Own Support (1982) NAYC, UK

Creative Training (1982) NAYC, UK

Help! Finding and Keeping Volunteers (1983) NAYC, UK

Partners (1985) Northamptonshire County Council, UK

Listening Power (1988) Management Learning Resources, UK

Show What You Know (1989) NYB, UK

Learning from Experience: building a learning organization (1990) Employment Department: Learning Technologies Unit, UK

Portfolios for Development (1994) Kogan Page, UK and Nichols Publishing, USA

Achieving Personal Success: an introduction to Inner Balancing (1995) Merlin Star Press, Canada

Counselling Your Staff (1995) Kogan Page, UK. Portuguese translation Clio Editoria, Brazil

Facilitation Skills for Team Development (1996) Kogan Page, UK. Portuguese translation Clio Editoria, Brazil

The 9 Steps to Emotional Fitness: a tool-kit for life in the 21st century (2003) Merlin Star Press, Canada

MORE RECIPES

SEND US YOUR RECIPES!

Now that you have read *Recipes for Inner Peace*, I invite you to be part of *More Recipes for Inner Peace*. Send in your own, both from your life experiences and your favorite healthy food recipes.

Write down your story – in no more than 500 words, adding your food recipe, and it will be considered for the next book. Imagine having your personal recipe for inner peace published in a book. You will be able to show all your family and friends, bringing to them a greater sense of who you are and the opportunity for them to experience some of that inner peace. People from around the world will see your message.

Send your entries to "More Recipes for Inner Peace" to me via e-mail to info@InnerBalancing.com or check out the Website at www.RecipesforInnerPeace.com.

Make sure you include your name and all contact details on your entry. Share your wisdom and experience with a waiting world.

To send this book to your family or friends, please see the ordering information on reverse.

Grilled Portabello Mushrooms

Cooking at high heat caramelizes the vinegar and turns this meaty mushroom into a real winner.

Estimated Times:
Preparation Time: 10 mins
Cook Time: 10 mins

Servings: 3

Ingredients

1 tablespoon olive oil
1 tablespoon balsamic vinegar
1/2 pound fresh portabello mushrooms
1/8 teaspoon salt
1 dash ground black pepper

Directions

MIX olive oil and balsamic vinegar.

BRUSH lightly over mushroom surface.

SEASON with salt and pepper.

GRILL, roast or broil until tender and golden brown.

Ordering Information

Illustrates with elegance and ease, how to live life happily.
BULK DISCOUNTS AVAILABLE.

Please call us toll-free at 1-866-310-EFit (3348)

Please fill out this form and fax to (403) 229-1850, e-mail to: warren@innerbalancing.com or mail with check to:

Centre for Inner Balancing
348 - 5th Avenue N.E. Calgary, Alberta, Canada T2E 0K8
***Please make checks payable to: Centre for Inner Balancing

Please rush me ____ copies of Recipes for Inner Peace
@ $15 CDN (or $12 US)   = $ _____

Postage & Handling ____ items @ $3/item (CDN or US) = $ _____
7% GST for Canadian orders   = $ _____

TOTAL - please check either ☐ CDN $ or ☐ US $ = $ _____

www.RecipesforInnerPeace.com You can also order online at

Ship to (Name:) _____
Organization: _____
Address: _____
City: _____ State/Province: _____
Country: _____ Zip/P.C.: _____
Phone: _____ Fax: _____
E-mail: _____

☐ *Yes,* I would like to receive the Equilibrium, Centre for Inner Balancing's monthly e-newsletter. You may also join by visiting:
www.RecipesforInnerPeace.com.

Ordering Information

**$24.99 CDN
($19.99 US)**

$14.95 CDN
($11.26 US)

Other books available to order.

Please call us toll-free at 1-866-310-EFit (3348)

Please fill out this form and fax to (403) 229-1850, e-mail to: warren@innerbalancing.com or mail with check to: **Centre for Inner Balancing** 348 - 5th Avenue N.E. Calgary, Alberta, Canada T2E 0K8

Please make checks payable to: Centre for Inner Balancing

Title	Quantity	Price	Total
The 9 Steps to Emotional Fitness		$24.99 CDN $19.99 US	
Achieving Personal Success		$14.95 CDN $11.26 US	
Shipping/Handling: $3/item (CDN or US)			
Subtotal			
7% GST (Canada only)			
Total Enclosed			

Deliver to:

Ship to (Name:) ——————————————

Organization: ————————————————

Address: ———————————————————

City: ———————— State/Province: ——————

Country: ———————— Zip/P.C.: ——————————

Phone: ———————— Fax: ————————————

E-mail: ——————————————————————

You can also order online at www.InnerBalancing.com

For personal coaching, or training to become an
Emotional Fitness Coach,
contact the Centre for Inner Balancing.
www.InnerBalancing.com